This book is dedicated to my mother, my partner Thomas, and my grandparents for all their support, feedback, and inspiration making this book.

Bamboo & Magnolias: Southern Comfort and Asian Fusion Recipes for the Adventurous Palate

By Austin Lubetkin

Cooking, for many, is a daily necessity, but for some, it becomes a profound form of self-expression and discovery. Throughout my life I've always felt like man with a fork in a world of soup, through it all cooking has been my steadfast peer. It's a journey that began in the quiet sanctity of my mother's kitchen, a place where the rhythmic rituals of chopping and stirring seemed to quiet the noisy chaos that often crowded my mind. My mother, a maestro of the culinary arts, introduced me to the intricacies of French and Southern Comfort cuisine, intertwining it seamlessly with our Jewish heritage. From her, I learned that cooking was more than the preparation of nourishment; it was an art form I could process my emotions in tangible, flavorful forms.

As a home cook on the autism spectrum, the kitchen became my sanctuary during the global pandemic. I had just started my adult life after moving across the country away from those I often shared a table with. Those days, filled with uncertainty and isolation, allowed me to grow under the responsibility of living and cooking on my own and became an opportunity to focus on developing my culinary techniques. It became a daily ritual that not only fed the body but also healed the soul. Food became a way to make it easier to connect with others and those many shared meals with neighbors and friends helped open up to the world at a time when connection felt all but lost.

Los Angeles, with its tapestry of cultures and cuisines, was where my culinary canvas expanded. I've always loved Asian cuisine, yet being in Los Angeles I had opportunities where I could try authentic dishes I'd never seen before while also having access to the ingredients to practice and learn to cook the dishes I grew fond of. This exposure was not just an expansion of my palate but an opening of my world. The city, vibrant and pulsating with diverse life, taught me to appreciate the richness of blending seemingly disparate elements, both in cuisine and in life.

This cookbook is a reflection of that journey—a fusion of Southern comfort, and the bold flavors of Asia. I explore ways to combine the flavors, dishes, and spices I'm passionate about. Through life, I've never tried to limit myself. Autism can be a gift because it has allowed me to chase my creativity without limiting myself or questioning what is expected of a meal. I could love sushi and fried chicken and didn't think twice about marrying the two. These recipes are a culinary love letter to eating the food you love and inspiring others to look at food from the lens of passion instead of expectation.

Through this collection, I invite you to explore the synthesis of traditions and tastes that define my cooking style. Here, you'll find dishes crafted not only to satisfy the taste buds but to stir the soul, much like the way my mother's cooking stirred my own creative spirit. Cooking, I've learned, is a powerful medium through which we can connect with others, share our stories, and express our most authentic selves.

As you delve into these recipes, I hope you discover not just the joy of cooking but the joy of creating. May this book inspire you to experiment with flavors, to gather your loved ones around the dinner table, and to find comfort in the shared experience of a meal well made. After all, cooking is more than creating food—it's about creating moments, memories, and sometimes, a much-needed bridge to the world around us.

APPETIZERS

Pimento Cheese Rangoon & Asian Fusion Ranch

Difficulty: Easy

Flavor Profile: A delightful fusion of creamy, cheesy Southern flavors encased in a crispy wonton, served with a unique Asian-inspired Ranch dipping sauce.

This recipe for Pimento Cheese Rangoon with Asian Fusion Ranch Dipping Sauce blends traditional Southern flavors with Asian influences, creating a unique and tasty appetizer perfect for parties or family gatherings.

Tips:
- Crispiness Tip: Ensure the oil is hot enough before frying to get a crispy texture without absorbing too much oil.
- Sealing the Wontons: Double seal by pressing down with the tines of a fork along the edges of the wontons after folding. This technique helps prevent the filling from leaking out during frying.
- Sauce Consistency: For a thinner sauce, add a little more buttermilk; for a thicker sauce, increase the mayonnaise or sour cream.

Ingredients:

- *For the Pimento Cheese Rangoon:*
  - 1 cup sharp cheddar cheese, shredded
  - 1/4 cup mayonnaise
  - 2 tablespoons diced pimentos
  - 1 teaspoon garlic powder
  - 1 teaspoon onion powder
  - 24 wonton wrappers
  - Oil for frying

- *For the Asian Fusion Ranch Dipping Sauce:*
  - 1 cup mayonnaise
  - 1/2 cup sour cream
  - 1/4 cup buttermilk
  - 2 tablespoons finely chopped green onions
  - 1 tablespoon finely chopped cilantro
  - 1 clove garlic, minced
  - 1 tablespoon lime juice
  - 1 teaspoon fish sauce
  - 1 teaspoon soy sauce
  - 1/2 teaspoon sesame oil
  - 1 tablespoon finely chopped pickled ginger
  - 1/2 teaspoon sugar
  - Salt and pepper to taste
  - Optional: 1 teaspoon sriracha or chili sauce for extra heat

Instructions:

1. Prepare the Filling:
   - In a mixing bowl, combine the shredded cheddar cheese, mayonnaise, diced pimentos, garlic powder, and onion powder. Stir until well blended and smooth.

2. Fill the Wontons:
   - Lay out the wonton wrappers on a clean surface. Place about one teaspoon of the pimento cheese mixture in the center of each wrapper.
   - Moisten the edges of each wrapper with a little water using your finger or a small brush. Fold the wrappers over the filling to form triangles, pressing the edges firmly to seal and eliminate any air pockets.

Instructions Continued:

3. Fry the Wontons:
   - Heat oil in a deep fryer or a large, heavy-bottomed pot to 350°F (175°C). Fry the wontons in batches, without overcrowding, until golden brown and crispy, about 2-3 minutes per side.
   - Use a slotted spoon to remove the wontons and drain them on paper towels.

4. Prepare the Asian Fusion Ranch Dipping Sauce:
   - In a medium bowl, whisk together mayonnaise, sour cream, and buttermilk until smooth.
   - Add green onions, cilantro, minced garlic, lime juice, fish sauce, soy sauce, sesame oil, and pickled ginger. Stir to combine thoroughly.
   - Stir in the sugar, and if desired, the sriracha or chili sauce for an extra kick.
   - Season the sauce with salt and pepper. Adjust the flavor as needed to balance the tangy, sweet, and spicy elements.

5. Chill the Sauce:
   - Cover the sauce and refrigerate for at least one hour to allow the flavors to meld. This step enhances the depth and harmony of the different taste components.

6. Serve:
   - Arrange the fried Pimento Cheese Rangoon on a serving platter. Serve alongside the chilled Asian Fusion Ranch Dipping Sauce.
   - Garnish the sauce with a sprinkle of chopped cilantro or green onions for a fresh, colorful presentation.

Nashville Hot Chicken Rice Paper Dumplings

Difficulty: Medium

Flavor Profile: These crispy rice paper dumplings combine the fiery, bold flavors of Nashville Hot Chicken with a satisfying crunch from the rice paper wrapper. The filling is spicy, savory, and tender, while the rice paper crisps up perfectly when pan-fried, creating a delightful fusion of Southern heat and Asian technique.

This Nashville Hot Chicken Rice Paper Dumplings recipe combines the crispy goodness of fried rice paper with the bold, spicy flavors of Nashville hot chicken, creating a fusion dish that's perfect for those who love heat with a satisfying crunch!

Tips:

- Rice Paper Handling: Soak the rice paper just until pliable. Over-soaking can make it too fragile and difficult to work with.
- Frying: Fry the dumplings over medium heat to avoid burning the delicate rice paper. A shallow fry is sufficient to achieve a crispy texture.
- Adjusting Heat: If you prefer a milder version, reduce the amount of cayenne pepper and Nashville hot sauce, or offer a cooling dip like ranch on the side to balance the heat.

Ingredients:

- For the Nashville Hot Chicken Filling:
- 2 boneless, skinless chicken breasts, cooked and shredded
- 2 tablespoons Nashville hot sauce (or hot sauce of your choice)
- 1 tablespoon paprika
- 1 teaspoon cayenne pepper (adjust for heat level)
- 1 teaspoon garlic powder
- 1 teaspoon onion powder
- 1 tablespoon brown sugar
- 1/4 teaspoon black pepper
- 1/4 cup mayonnaise (optional, for a creamier filling)
- Salt to taste

- For the Dumplings:
- 10-12 rice paper sheets
- Warm water (for softening the rice paper)
- Vegetable oil (for frying)

- For Serving:
- Pickles (optional, for serving)
- Ranch or blue cheese dressing (optional, for dipping)
- Fresh chopped herbs (optional garnish)

Instructions:

1. Prepare the Nashville Hot Chicken Filling:
- Cook and shred the chicken breasts if not already done. Set aside.
- In a large bowl, mix together the Nashville hot sauce, paprika, cayenne pepper, garlic powder, onion powder, brown sugar, and black pepper.
- Add the shredded chicken to the spice mixture and toss until the chicken is fully coated. For a creamier filling, stir in the mayonnaise.
- Taste the filling and adjust seasoning with salt if necessary.

Instructions Continued:

2. Assemble the Rice Paper Dumplings:
   - Prepare a shallow bowl or pie dish with warm water.
   - Working one at a time, dip each rice paper sheet into the warm water for 5-10 seconds, until soft but not overly soggy.
   - Place the softened rice paper on a clean surface and add 2-3 tablespoons of the Nashville hot chicken filling in the center of the rice paper.
   - Fold the sides of the rice paper over the filling and then roll it up tightly like a burrito to form a dumpling. Set aside and repeat with the remaining rice paper sheets and filling.

3. Fry the Dumplings:
   - Heat a large skillet over medium heat and add enough vegetable oil to coat the bottom of the pan.
   - Once the oil is hot, carefully add the dumplings in batches. Cook for about 2-3 minutes on each side, or until the rice paper is crispy and golden brown. Be sure to watch them closely, as rice paper can burn quickly.
   - Remove the dumplings from the skillet and drain on a paper towel-lined plate.

4. Serve:
   - Serve the Nashville Hot Chicken Rice Paper Dumplings with pickles, ranch or blue cheese dressing for dipping, and a garnish of fresh herbs if desired.
   - These dumplings are best enjoyed hot and crispy!

Rice Paper Wrapped Grits Fries with Hoisin Ketchup Dipping Sauce

Difficulty: Medium

Flavor Profile: These crispy grits fries wrapped in rice paper have a delightful crunch on the outside and creamy, savory grits on the inside. Paired with a sweet and tangy hoisin ketchup dipping sauce, this fusion dish is a unique take on Southern and Asian flavors.

These Rice Paper Wrapped Grits Fries are a perfect fusion of Southern comfort food and Asian street food, providing a fun and flavorful twist on the classic fries with a crunchy exterior and creamy interior, perfectly complemented by the tangy-sweet hoisin ketchup dipping sauce!

Tips:
- Crispiness: Be sure to fry the grits fries over medium heat to prevent burning the rice paper. It should be golden brown and crispy on the outside, with the grits remaining creamy inside.
- Rice Paper Wrapping: Wrap the fries tightly in rice paper to prevent the grits from spilling out during frying.
- Variations: For an extra twist, you can sprinkle the grits with Cajun seasoning or smoked paprika before wrapping for a spicier flavor.

Ingredients:

- For the Grits Fries:

- 1 cup stone-ground grits
- 4 cups water (or chicken broth for extra flavor)
- 1 tablespoon butter
- 1/2 cup sharp cheddar cheese (optional)
- Salt and pepper to taste
- 10-12 rice paper sheets
- Vegetable oil (for frying)

- For the Hoisin Ketchup Dipping Sauce:

- 1/4 cup ketchup
- 2 tablespoons hoisin sauce
- 1 tablespoon rice vinegar
- 1 teaspoon soy sauce
- 1 teaspoon sriracha (optional for heat)
- 1/2 teaspoon sesame oil

Instructions:

1. Prepare the Grits:

   - In a medium saucepan, bring the water (or chicken broth) to a boil. Slowly whisk in the grits, reduce the heat to low, and cook for about 20-25 minutes, stirring frequently, until the grits are thick and creamy.
   - Stir in the butter, cheddar cheese (if using), and season with salt and pepper to taste. Cook until the cheese is melted and the grits are smooth.
   - Spread the cooked grits into a greased baking dish or on a parchment-lined baking sheet to a thickness of about 1/2 inch. Let the grits cool completely in the fridge for at least 1 hour or until firm.

2. Cut the Grits:

   - Once the grits have set, remove them from the fridge and cut them into rectangular fry shapes, about 3 inches long and 1/2 inch thick.

Instructions Continued:

3. Wrap the Grits Fries in Rice Paper:

- Fill a shallow dish with warm water. Soak one rice paper sheet at a time in the water for 5-10 seconds, until softened.
- Place the softened rice paper on a clean surface and put one grits fry at the edge of the rice. paperRoll the fry up tightly in the rice paper, folding in the sides as you roll to create a neat package. Repeat with the remaining grits fries.

4. Fry the Grits Fries:

- Heat about 1/4 inch of vegetable oil in a large skillet over medium heat. Once the oil is hot, carefully add the rice paper-wrapped grits fries in batches.
- Fry for about 2-3 minutes on each side, or until the rice paper is golden brown and crispy. Be careful not to overcrowd the pan.
- Transfer the fried grits fries to a paper towel-lined plate to drain any excess oil.

5. Make the Hoisin Ketchup Dipping Sauce:

- In a small bowl, whisk together the ketchup, hoisin sauce, rice vinegar, soy sauce, sriracha (if using), and sesame oil until smooth. Adjust seasoning to taste if needed.

6. Serve:

- Arrange the crispy rice paper-wrapped grits fries on a serving plate and serve alongside the hoisin ketchup dipping sauce.
- Garnish with chopped green onions or sesame seeds for added flavor and presentation, if desired.

Smoked Gouda and Kimchi Croquettes

Difficulty: Medium

Flavor Profile: These croquettes offer a delightful combination of creamy, smoky Gouda cheese and tangy, spicy kimchi, all encased in a crispy, golden breadcrumb coating. Perfect for a fusion appetizer that packs a punch of flavor.

Smoked Gouda and Kimchi Croquettes blend the creamy texture of cheese with the zest of kimchi in a snack that's ideal for parties or as a bold appetizer before a main meal, offering a fusion of Korean and Western tastes that are sure to delight the palate.

Tips:
- Consistency of Mixture: Ensure the potato mixture is not too wet; it should be firm enough to hold its shape when formed. If the mixture is too loose, add a little more mashed potato or some breadcrumbs to help bind it.
- Kimchi Selection: Use well-fermented kimchi for a stronger flavor. Ensure it is drained well to prevent excess moisture from affecting the mixture.
- Breading: Double-breading the croquettes by repeating the egg and breadcrumb steps can ensure a thicker, crunchier exterior.

Ingredients:

- For the Croquette Filling:
  - 2 cups mashed potatoes, cooled
  - 1 cup smoked Gouda cheese, finely grated
  - 1 cup kimchi, drained and finely chopped
  - 2 green onions, finely sliced
  - 1 teaspoon garlic powder
  - Salt and pepper to taste

- For Breading and Frying:
  - 1 cup all-purpose flour
  - 2 large eggs, beaten
  - 2 cups panko breadcrumbs
  - Oil for frying

- For Serving:
  - Sour cream or a spicy mayo for dipping
  - Chopped chives or parsley for garnish

Instructions:

1. Prepare the Croquette Mixture:
    - In a large bowl, combine the mashed potatoes, smoked Gouda, finely chopped kimchi, green onions, and garlic powder. Season with salt and pepper to taste.
    - Mix thoroughly until all ingredients are well incorporated. Taste and adjust seasoning if necessary.

2. Shape the Croquettes:
    - With clean hands, shape the mixture into small, oval or round balls. Each should be about the size of a golf ball.

3. Set Up Breading Station:
    - Prepare three shallow bowls: one for the flour, one for the beaten eggs, and one for the panko breadcrumbs.
    - Roll each croquette first in the flour, shaking off excess, then dip into the beaten eggs, and finally coat thoroughly with the panko breadcrumbs. Set aside on a tray.

Instructions Continued:

4. Fry the Croquettes:
   - Heat oil in a deep fryer or a large, deep skillet to 350°F (175°C).
   - Fry the croquettes in batches, being careful not to overcrowd the pan, until golden brown and crispy, about 3-4 minutes.
   - Use a slotted spoon to transfer the croquettes to a plate lined with paper towels to drain excess oil.

5. Serve:
   - Serve the croquettes hot, garnished with chopped chives or parsley.
   - Provide sour cream, spicy mayo, or fusion ranch for dipping.

Szechuan Crab Cakes with Jalapeño Remoulade

Difficulty: Medium

Flavor Profile: These crab cakes feature a tantalizing blend of sweet crab meat and fiery Szechuan spices, complemented by a spicy and tangy jalapeño remoulade.

Szechuan Crab Cakes with Jalapeño Remoulade offer a delightful fusion of East meets South, with each bite delivering a burst of spicy, savory, and tangy flavors that are sure to impress any palate.

Tips:

- Handling Crab Meat: Handle the crab meat gently to keep the pieces as intact as possible for a better texture in the crab cakes.
- Szechuan Chili Paste Adjustment: Adjust the amount of Szechuan chili paste according to your spice preference. Start with less and add more as needed.
- Serving Suggestions: These crab cakes make an excellent starter for a dinner party or can be served as a light main course paired with a fresh salad or steamed vegetables.

Ingredients:

- *For the Crab Cakes*:

  - 1 pound lump crab meat, picked over for shells
  - 1/2 cup panko breadcrumbs, plus extra for coating
  - 1/4 cup minced green onions
  - 1 egg, beaten
  - 2 tablespoons mayonnaise
  - 1 tablespoon Szechuan chili paste
  - 1 teaspoon minced garlic
  - 1 teaspoon grated ginger
  - 1 tablespoon soy sauce
  - 1 teaspoon sesame oil
  - Salt and pepper to taste
  - Vegetable oil, for frying

- *For the Jalapeño Remoulade*:

  - 1 cup mayonnaise
  - 1 medium jalapeño, seeded and finely chopped
  - 2 tablespoons capers, chopped
  - 2 tablespoons chopped parsley
  - 1 tablespoon Dijon mustard
  - 1 tablespoon lemon juice
  - 1 teaspoon paprika
  - Salt and pepper to taste

Instructions:

1. Prepare the Crab Cakes:
   - In a large bowl, combine the crab meat, panko breadcrumbs, green onions, egg, mayonnaise, Szechuan chili paste, garlic, ginger, soy sauce, and sesame oil. Gently mix until well combined, being careful not to break up the crab meat too much. Season with salt and pepper to taste.
   - Shape the mixture into patties, about 3 inches in diameter and 1/2 inch thick. Coat each patty lightly with additional panko breadcrumbs.
   - Refrigerate the crab cakes for at least 30 minutes to firm up.

2. Make the Jalapeño Remoulade:
   - In a mixing bowl, combine mayonnaise, chopped jalapeño, capers, parsley, Dijon mustard, lemon juice, and paprika. Stir until well blended. Season with salt and pepper to taste. Chill in the refrigerator until ready to serve.

Instructions Continued:

3. Cook the Crab Cakes:
   - Heat a thin layer of vegetable oil in a large skillet over medium heat. Carefully place the crab cakes in the skillet and fry until golden brown and crispy, about 4-5 minutes per side.
   - Transfer the crab cakes to a plate lined with paper towels to drain excess oil.

4. Serve:
   - Arrange the crab cakes on a serving platter or individual plates.
   - Serve with a dollop of jalapeño remoulade on the side or spooned over the top of each crab cake.
   - Garnish with additional green onions or parsley if desired.

Spicy Miso Eggplant Dip

Difficulty: Easy

Flavor Profile: This dip combines the smoky depth of roasted eggplant with the umami-rich flavor of miso and a kick of spice, creating a bold and complex appetizer perfect for dipping or spreading.

A versatile and crowd-pleasing appetizer that's also easy to make. The preparation is both easy and forgiving.

Tips:

- Eggplant Preparation: You don't have to worry about over cooking the eggplant since any additional char helps develop a deep, smoky flavor which is crucial for this dip.
- Adjusting Spiciness: The level of heat can be customized by adjusting the amount of sriracha sauce. Start with a small amount and increase according to your spice preference.
- Storage: This dip can be stored in an airtight container in the refrigerator for up to 4 days. Stir well before serving as separation may occur.

Ingredients:

- *For the Dip:*
  - 2 large eggplants
  - 2 tablespoons olive oil
  - 3 tablespoons red miso paste
  - 1 tablespoon tahini (sesame paste)
  - 2 cloves garlic, minced

Ingredients Continued:

- 1 tablespoon fresh ginger, grated
- 1 tablespoon soy sauce
- 2 teaspoons sriracha sauce, or to taste
- 1 tablespoon lime juice
- 1 teaspoon sesame oil
- Salt and pepper, to taste

- *For Garnish*:
  - 1 tablespoon sesame seeds, toasted
  - 2 green onions, thinly sliced
  - Fresh cilantro, chopped (optional)

Instructions:

1. Roast the Eggplants:
   - Preheat your oven to 400°F (200°C).
   - Pierce the eggplants several times with a fork and brush them with olive oil.
   - Place the eggplants on a baking sheet lined with parchment paper, and roast in the oven until they are completely soft and the skins are charred, about 30-40 minutes.
   - Remove from the oven and let cool. Once cool enough to handle, peel off the skin and scoop out the soft flesh.

2. Make the Dip:
   - In a food processor, combine the roasted eggplant flesh, miso paste, tahini, minced garlic, grated ginger, soy sauce, sriracha sauce, lime juice, and sesame oil.
   - Process until the mixture is smooth and creamy. Taste and adjust seasoning with salt and pepper.

3. Chill and Serve:
   - Transfer the dip to a serving bowl and refrigerate for at least 1 hour to allow the flavors to meld together.
   - Before serving, sprinkle the top with toasted sesame seeds, sliced green onions, and chopped cilantro if using.

4. Serving Suggestions:
   - Serve the dip with a variety of crackers, sliced baguette, or fresh vegetables such as cucumber slices, carrot sticks, or bell pepper strips.
   - This dip can also be used as a spread for sandwiches or wraps to enhance the flavor of other ingredients.

Thai Basil and Peach Bruschetta

Difficulty: Easy

Flavor Profile: A delightful combination of aromatic Thai basil and the sweet juiciness of peaches, served on crispy toasted bread.

This Thai Basil and Peach Bruschetta recipe effortlessly combines Southern and Asian influences, creating a light yet flavorful appetizer that's as perfect for a casual get-together as it is for a more formal gathering.

Tips:
- Choosing Peaches: Opt for peaches that are ripe for natural sweetness yet firm enough to hold their shape when diced. This texture contrast is key to the perfect bruschetta topping.
- Alternative Sweeteners: If you prefer a vegan option, you can substitute honey with agave syrup or a small amount of maple syrup.
- Serving Suggestion: These bruschettas make an excellent starter for a summer dinner party or as a part of a tapas-style spread. They pair wonderfully with a chilled glass of Riesling or a light sparkling wine, which complements the fruity and herby flavors.

Ingredients:

- 1 baguette, cut into 1/2-inch slices
- 2 large peaches, finely diced
- 1/4 cup fresh Thai basil leaves, roughly chopped, plus extra for garnish
- 2 tablespoons red onion, finely minced
- 1 tablespoon fresh lime juice
- 1 teaspoon fish sauce
- 1 teaspoon honey
- Salt and freshly ground black pepper to taste
- Olive oil for brushing

Instructions:

1. Prepare the Baguette:
   - Preheat your oven to 375°F (190°C).
   - Lightly brush each baguette slice with olive oil on both sides. Arrange the slices in a single layer on a baking sheet.
   - Toast in the oven for about 5-7 minutes, or until the edges are golden brown and crisp. Flip each slice halfway through to ensure even toasting.

2. Mix the Topping:
   - In a mixing bowl, combine the diced peaches, chopped Thai basil, minced red onion, lime juice, fish sauce, and honey.
   - Season the mixture with salt and pepper to taste. Stir gently to combine all the ingredients without breaking the peach pieces.
   - Allow the mixture to sit for about 10 minutes to let the flavors meld together. This resting period helps the peaches absorb the aromatic and tangy elements of the marinade.

3. Assemble the Bruschetta:
   - Once the baguette slices are toasted and slightly cooled, spoon a generous amount of the peach-basil topping onto each slice.
   - Make sure to distribute the mixture evenly, allowing a bit of juice to soak into the bread without making it soggy.

4. Serve:
   - Arrange the bruschetta on a serving platter. Garnish with additional Thai basil leaves for an extra touch of freshness and color.
   - Serve immediately while the bread is still crisp and the topping is fresh.

Sesame Fried Okra

Difficulty: Advanced

Flavor Profile: Crispy and golden fried okra with a sticky, sweet, and slightly spicy sesame sauce, reminiscent of the popular Chinese sesame chicken.

This Sesame Fried Okra recipe takes a Southern favorite and dresses it up with the rich, nutty flavors of a classic Asian sesame sauce, creating a delicious fusion dish that's perfect for sharing or as a unique addition to any meal.

Tips:
- Frying in Batches: Ensure not to overcrowd the pot while frying to keep the okra crispy.
- Serving Suggestions: Serve as an appetizer with dipping sauces or as a side dish to complement grilled meats or a vegetable stir-fry.
- Adjusting Spiciness: Control the heat by adjusting the amount of red pepper flakes, or omit them for a milder flavor.

Ingredients:
- *For the Fried Okra:*
  - 1 lb fresh okra
  - 1 cup buttermilk
  - 1 cup all-purpose flour
  - 1 cup cornstarch
  - 1 teaspoon salt
  - 1 teaspoon pepper
  - Oil for frying

- *For the Sesame Sauce:*
  - 1/4 cup soy sauce
  - 1/4 cup honey
  - 2 tablespoons brown sugar
  - 2 tablespoons rice vinegar
  - 1 tablespoon sesame oil
  - 2 cloves garlic, minced
  - 1 teaspoon grated ginger
  - 1 tablespoon cornstarch mixed with 2 tablespoons water (slurry)
  - 2 tablespoons toasted sesame seeds
  - 1/4 teaspoon red pepper flakes (optional)

- *Garnish*:
  - Additional toasted sesame seeds
  - Thinly sliced green onions

Instructions:
1. Prepare the Okra:
   - Slice the okra into about ¾ inch pieces. Discard the stems and skinny tips
   - Soak the sliced okra in buttermilk for at least 30 minutes. This step helps tenderize the okra and provides a tangy flavor that enhances the batter.

2. Heat the Oil:
   - In a deep fryer or large pot, heat oil to 375°F (190°C).

Instructions Continued:

3. Dredge and Fry the Okra:
    - In a mixing bowl, combine flour, cornstarch, salt, and pepper.
    - Remove okra from buttermilk, allowing excess to drip off.
    - Dredge okra slices in the flour mixture until they are well coated.
    - Fry in batches in the hot oil until golden brown and crispy, about 2-3 minutes. Remove with a slotted   spoon and drain on paper towels.

4. Make the Sesame Sauce:
    - In a small saucepan over medium heat, combine soy sauce, honey, brown sugar, and rice vinegar.
    - Bring to a simmer.
    - Add minced garlic, grated ginger, and sesame oil, stirring to incorporate.
    - Add the cornstarch slurry to the saucepan, stirring constantly until the sauce thickens, about 1-2 minutes.
    - Stir in toasted sesame seeds and red pepper flakes if using.

5. Coat the Fried Okra:
    - In a large bowl, toss the crispy fried okra with the sesame sauce until evenly coated.

6. Serve:
    - Plate the sesame fried okra. Garnish with additional toasted sesame seeds and thinly sliced green onions.
    - Serve immediately to maintain the crispiness of the okra.

Sweet Chili Cornbread with Wasabi Peas Crust

Difficulty: Medium

Flavor Profile: A unique combination of sweet, spicy, and tangy flavors, this cornbread features a vibrant sweet chili infusion complemented by a crunchy, zesty wasabi peas crust.

This Sweet Chili Cornbread with Wasabi Peas Crust combines traditional Southern cooking with bold Asian flavors, creating a unique and delicious twist on classic cornbread. It's perfect for those who enjoy a little adventure in their culinary explorations.

Tips:

- Texture of Cornbread: For a moister cornbread, you can add a small can of creamed corn to the batter.
- Serving Suggestions: This cornbread pairs wonderfully with soups, stews, or as a unique side to a salad.
- Wasabi Peas: Ensure the wasabi peas are finely crushed to create a consistent crust and to avoid overly large chunks, which can be overpowering.

Ingredients:

- For the Cornbread:
  - 1 cup all-purpose flour
  - 1 cup yellow cornmeal
  - 1/4 cup granulated sugar
  - 1 tablespoon baking powder
  - 1/2 teaspoon salt
  - 2/3 cup milk
  - 1/3 cup plain greek yogurt
  - 2 large eggs
  - 1/4 cup vegetable oil
  - 1/4 cup sweet chili sauce

- For the Wasabi Peas Crust:
  - 1 cup wasabi peas, crushed into coarse crumbs
  - 2 tablespoons melted butter

- For the Sweet Chili Glaze:
  - 1/4 cup sweet chili sauce
  - 2 tablespoons honey
  - Juice of 1 lime

Instructions:

1. Preheat the Oven and Prepare the Pan:
   - Preheat your oven to 375°F (190°C).
   - Grease an 8-inch square baking dish or a similar sized cast iron skillet.

2. Mix the Dry Ingredients:
   - In a large mixing bowl, whisk together the flour, cornmeal, sugar, baking powder, and salt.

Instructions Continued:

3. Combine the Wet Ingredients:
   - In a separate bowl, beat the milk, greek yogurt, eggs, vegetable oil, and 1/4 cup sweet chili sauce until well combined.

4. Make the Cornbread Batter:
   - Add the wet ingredients to the dry ingredients, stirring just until the dry ingredients are moistened and everything is evenly combined. Avoid over mixing to keep the cornbread tender.

5. Prepare the Wasabi Peas Crust:
   - In a small bowl, mix the crushed wasabi peas with melted butter until the mixture resembles coarse crumbs.

6. Assemble and Bake:
   - Pour the cornbread batter into the prepared baking dish.
   - Evenly sprinkle the wasabi peas mixture over the top of the batter, pressing lightly to adhere.
   - Bake in the preheated oven for 25-30 minutes, or until a toothpick inserted in the center comes out clean.

7. Prepare the Sweet Chili Glaze:
   - While the cornbread is baking, whisk together 1/4 cup sweet chili sauce, honey, and lime juice in a small saucepan.
   - Heat over medium heat until the mixture is heated through and slightly thickened.

8. Finish and Serve:
   - Remove the cornbread from the oven and immediately brush the top with the warm sweet chili glaze.
   - Let the cornbread cool in the pan for at least 10 minutes before slicing.
   - Serve warm, ideally with a side of butter or extra sweet chili sauce for dipping.

Kimchi Deviled Eggs

Difficulty: Easy

Flavor Profile: A tangy and spicy twist on classic deviled eggs, infused with the bold flavors of kimchi and a hint of sesame.

These Kimchi Deviled Eggs are an innovative and flavorful take on a traditional party favorite, combining creamy, spicy, and umami elements into each bite. They are sure to be a hit with guests looking for something uniquely delicious!

Tips:
- Egg Peeling Tip: Older eggs peel more easily than fresh ones, so consider using eggs that have been in your fridge for a week or so.
- Spice Level: Adjust the amount of kimchi and kimchi juice according to your spice tolerance. More kimchi juice will make the filling tangier and spicier.
- Serving Suggestion: Kimchi deviled eggs make a great appetizer for parties and can be paired with other Asian-inspired dishes or a selection of appetizers for a diverse flavor experience.

Ingredients:
- *For the Eggs:*
  - 12 large eggs
  - Ice water

Ingredients Continued:

- *For the Filling:*
  - 1/2 cup finely chopped kimchi
  - 1/4 cup mayonnaise
  - 1 tablespoon kimchi juice (from the kimchi container)
  - 1 teaspoon sesame oil
  - 1/2 teaspoon sugar
  - Salt and pepper to taste

- *Garnishes:*
  - Sesame seeds
  - Chopped green onions
  - Additional chopped kimchi

Instructions:

1. Cook the Eggs:
   - Place eggs in a large saucepan and cover them with cold water by 1 inch.
   - Bring to a boil over medium-high heat, then cover, turn off the heat, and let sit for 10 minutes.
   - Transfer the eggs to a bowl of ice water and let them cool completely. This stops the cooking process and makes the eggs easier to peel.

2. Prepare the Eggs:
   - Once cooled, peel the eggs and cut them in half lengthwise.
   - Carefully remove the yolks and place them in a separate bowl. Set the white halves on a serving platter.

3. Make the Filling:
   - Mash the yolks with a fork until they are crumbly.
   - Add the chopped kimchi, mayonnaise, kimchi juice, sesame oil, and sugar to the yolks. Mix until smooth and creamy.
   - Season the filling with salt and pepper to taste.

4. Fill the Eggs:
   - Spoon or pipe the filling back into the cavities of the egg whites. For a cleaner look, you can use a piping bag fitted with a star tip.

Instructions Continued:

5. Garnish and Serve:

   - Sprinkle each deviled egg with sesame seeds and chopped green onions.

   - Top each egg with a small piece of chopped kimchi for an additional flavor boost.

   - Chill in the refrigerator until ready to serve, preferably within a few hours for the best taste and texture.

Szechuan Hashbrown Casserole

Difficulty: Medium

Flavor Profile: Creamy and spicy with a bold Szechuan kick

This Szechuan Hashbrown Casserole offers a fiery twist on a traditional dish, perfect for those who enjoy a bit of heat with their comfort food. Its creamy texture and spicy notes make it an exciting addition to any meal, especially during cold weather or as a unique side dish at gatherings.

Optional Steps:
- For Less Spicy Version: Reduce the Szechuan peppercorns to 1 tablespoon and omit the chili oil. The casserole will still have a hint of warmth and numbing sensation without being overpowering.
- For Creamier Texture: Increase the amount of sour cream to 1 1/2 cups and add an extra 1/4 cup of milk to ensure the casserole stays moist and creamy during baking.

Ingredients:

- *Basic Ingredients:*

  - 2 lbs frozen shredded hashbrowns, thawed
  - 1 cup sour cream
  - 1 can (10.75 oz) cream of chicken soup
  - 2 cups shredded cheddar cheese
  - 1/2 cup melted butter
  - 1/2 cup milk
  - 1 medium onion, finely chopped
  - Salt and pepper to taste

- *Szechuan Ingredients:*

  - 2 tablespoons Szechuan peppercorns, crushed (use less for milder flavor)
  - 1 tablespoon chili oil (optional for extra heat)
  - 1 teaspoon garlic powder
  - 1 teaspoon ginger powder
  - 2 tablespoons soy sauce

- *Optional Toppings:*

  - 1/2 cup crushed Szechuan peppercorns (for a very spicy topping)
  - 1/2 cup breadcrumbs mixed with 2 tablespoons melted butter (for a crispy topping)
  - Additional chili oil or chili flakes to serve
  - Chopped up Bacon or Pork Belly

Instructions:

1. Preheat Oven:

   - Preheat your oven to 350°F (175°C). Grease a 9x13 inch baking dish.

2. Mix Ingredients:

   - In a large mixing bowl, combine the thawed hashbrowns, sour cream, cream of chicken soup, cheddar cheese, melted butter, and milk. Mix until well combined.
   - Stir in the chopped onion, garlic powder, ginger powder, and soy sauce. Add the crushed Szechuan peppercorns according to your spice preference.

3. Add Heat (Optional):

   - For additional heat, mix in chili oil into the hashbrown mixture. Adjust the amount based on how spicy you want the casserole to be.

Instructions Continued:

4. Transfer to Baking Dish:

    - Spoon the hashbrown mixture into the prepared baking dish, spreading evenly.

5. Add Optional Toppings:

    - If using, sprinkle a mix of crushed Szechuan peppercorns and breadcrumbs over the top of the casserole for extra spice and crunch. Alternatively, just use the breadcrumb mixture for a milder topping.

6. Bake:

    - Place the casserole in the oven and bake for 45-55 minutes or until the top is golden brown and crispy.

7. Serving:

    - Let the casserole sit for about 10 minutes after baking to set. Serve hot with a drizzle of chili oil or a sprinkle of chili flakes if you desire extra heat.

Baked Beans Bulgogi

Difficulty: Medium

Flavor Profile: This dish merges the hearty, comforting essence of Southern baked beans with the sweet and savory richness of Korean bulgogi. It's a delightful combination that offers a unique twist on two classic flavors.

Baked Beans Bulgogi is a perfect example of a successful fusion dish that combines traditional elements from both Southern and Korean cuisines, offering a rich, flavorful experience that is both comforting and exciting.

Tips:
- Marinating Time: The longer you marinate the beef, the more flavorful and tender the bulgogi will be.
- Serving Suggestions: This dish pairs well with steamed rice or a simple cucumber salad to balance the rich flavors.
- Customization: Feel free to adjust the level of sweetness or spiciness in the baked beans according to your taste by modifying the amounts of sugar, barbecue sauce, and chili powder.

Ingredients:

- *For the Bulgogi Marinade:*
  - 1 lb thinly sliced beef (ribeye or sirloin)
  - 1/4 cup soy sauce
  - 2 tablespoons brown sugar
  - 1 Asian pear, grated (acts as a tenderizer and sweetener)
  - 2 tablespoons sesame oil
  - 4 cloves garlic, minced
  - 1 inch piece of ginger, grated
  - 2 green onions, finely chopped
  - 1 tablespoon rice wine (mirin)
  - 1 teaspoon ground black pepper

- *For the Baked Beans:*
  - 2 cans (each 15 oz) navy beans, drained and rinsed
  - 1/2 cup barbecue sauce (choose a smoky variety for more depth)
  - 1/4 cup ketchup
  - 1/4 cup molasses
  - 1/4 cup brown sugar
  - 1 onion, diced
  - 1 red bell pepper, diced
  - 2 tablespoons apple cider vinegar
  - 1 teaspoon smoked paprika
  - 1/2 teaspoon chili powder
  - Salt and pepper to taste

Instructions:

1. Marinate the Beef:
   - In a bowl, combine soy sauce, brown sugar, grated Asian pear, sesame oil, minced garlic, grated ginger, chopped green onions, mirin, and black pepper to create the marinade.
   - Add the thinly sliced beef to the marinade, making sure each piece is well-coated. Cover and refrigerate for at least 1 hour, preferably overnight for deeper flavor.

Instructions Continued:

2. Prepare the Baked Beans:
   - Preheat your oven to 375°F (190°C).
   - In a large ovenproof skillet or Dutch oven, sauté the diced onion and red bell pepper until soft and translucent.
   - Stir in the barbecue sauce, ketchup, molasses, brown sugar, apple cider vinegar, smoked paprika, and chili powder. Mix well to combine.
   - Add the rinsed navy beans to the skillet, stirring until they are well coated with the sauce. Season with salt and pepper to taste.
   - Let the beans mixture simmer on the stovetop for about 10 minutes to meld the flavors.

3. Cook the Bulgogi:
   - While the beans are simmering, heat a large skillet over high heat. Add the marinated beef (in batches if necessary to avoid overcrowding) and cook for about 3-5 minutes, or until the meat is fully cooked and caramelized. Stir frequently to ensure even cooking and to prevent burning.

4. Combine and Bake:
   - If the beans were simmering in an ovenproof skillet, spread the cooked bulgogi over the beans. If not, transfer the beans to a baking dish and then top with the bulgogi.
   - Place the skillet or baking dish in the preheated oven and bake for 15-20 minutes, allowing the flavors to integrate fully.

5. Serve:
   - Remove from oven and let sit for a few minutes before serving.
   - Garnish with additional chopped green onions and a sprinkle of sesame seeds if desired.

Fusion Pho Nachos

Difficulty: Medium

Flavor Profile: A delightful blend of Vietnamese Pho flavors with the beloved Tex-Mex nachos, featuring pho-spiced beef, crispy tortilla chips, fresh herbs, and a zesty lime crema.

This innovative recipe for Fusion Pho Nachos creatively combines the aromatic spices and flavors of Vietnamese pho with the crunchy, cheesy delight of traditional nachos, creating a perfect dish for gatherings that bridge diverse culinary tastes.

Tips:
- Beef Preparation: Freezing the beef slightly will make it easier to slice thinly.
- Cheese Options: Feel free to experiment with different types of cheese that melt well, like cheddar or a Tex-Mex blend, to adjust the flavor profile.
- Serving Suggestion: These nachos are best enjoyed fresh from the oven. If serving at a party, consider setting up a nacho bar where guests can add their own toppings like additional herbs, lime wedges, and sauces.

Ingredients:

- *For the Pho Beef:*
  - 1 lb beef flank steak, thinly sliced
  - 1 tablespoon fish sauce
  - 1 tablespoon soy sauce
  - 1 clove garlic, minced
  - 1 teaspoon ginger, grated
  - 1/2 teaspoon five-spice powder
  - 1 teaspoon sugar

- *For the Lime Crema:*
  - 1/2 cup sour cream
  - Zest and juice of 1 lime
  - Salt to taste

- *For the Nachos:*
  - 8 oz tortilla chips
  - 1 cup mozzarella cheese, shredded
  - 1 cup Monterey Jack cheese, shredded
  - 1 jalapeño, thinly sliced
  - 1/2 red onion, finely chopped
  - 1/4 cup fresh cilantro, chopped
  - 1/4 cup Thai basil, chopped
  - 1/4 cup mint leaves, chopped
  - Bean sprouts (optional)
  - Hoisin sauce for drizzling
  - Sriracha sauce for drizzling

Instructions:

1. Marinate the Beef:
   - In a mixing bowl, combine the fish sauce, soy sauce, minced garlic, grated ginger, five-spice, powder and sugar. Stir well.
   - Add the thinly sliced beef to the marinade and ensure it is well coated. Let it marinate for at least 30 minutes in the refrigerator.

Instructions Continued:

2. Prepare the Lime Crema:
    - In a small bowl, mix together sour cream, lime zest, and lime juice. Season with a pinch of salt to taste. Set aside in the refrigerator.

3. Cook the Pho Beef:
    - Heat a skillet over medium-high heat. Remove the beef from the marinade, shaking off any excess, and stir-fry in the hot skillet until just cooked through, about 2-3 minutes. Set aside.

4. Assemble the Nachos:
    - Preheat your oven to 375°F (190°C).
    - Spread tortilla chips in a single layer on a large baking sheet or oven-safe platter.
    - Evenly distribute the cooked pho beef over the chips.
    - Sprinkle both types of cheese over the top, ensuring even coverage.
    - Scatter sliced jalapeños and chopped red onion over the cheese.
    - Bake in the preheated oven until the cheese is melted and bubbly, about 5-7 minutes.

5. Garnish and Serve:
    - Remove the nachos from the oven and immediately garnish with chopped cilantro, Thai basil, and mint leaves.
    - Add bean sprouts if using.
    - Drizzle hoisin sauce and sriracha over the top for extra flavor.
    - Dollop or drizzle lime crema across the nachos.
    - Serve immediately while hot and crispy.

Jalapeño and Soy Glazed Duck Tacos

Difficulty: Advanced

Flavor Profile: These tacos feature tender, flavorful duck with a sweet and spicy glaze, paired with the crunch of fresh vegetables and the warmth of soft tortillas, creating a unique fusion of Asian flavors and Mexican taco tradition.

These Jalapeño and Soy Glazed Duck Tacos offer a delightful combination of savory, sweet, and spicy flavors, making them a sophisticated yet fun choice for dinner parties, family meals, or any taco night looking for a gourmet twist.

Tips:
- Duck Cooking: Keep an eye on the duck as it cooks to ensure the skin doesn't burn. If the fat is rendering too quickly, reduce the heat slightly.
- Tortilla Options: While corn tortillas are suggested for their flavor and gluten-free properties, flour tortillas can also be used if preferred.
- Adjusting Heat: The heat level of the jalapeño soy glaze can be adjusted by using more or less jalapeño, or by adding a pinch of red pepper flakes for extra spice.

Ingredients:

- *For the Duck*:
  - 2 duck breasts, skin scored in a crosshatch pattern
  - Salt and pepper to taste

- *For the Jalapeño Soy Glaze:*
  - 1/4 cup soy sauce
  - 1/4 cup honey
  - 1 tablespoon rice vinegar
  - 2 tablespoons water
  - 1 jalapeño, finely chopped (remove seeds for less heat)
  - 2 cloves garlic, minced
  - 1 teaspoon grated ginger
  - 1 tablespoon cornstarch dissolved in 2 tablespoons cold water

- *For the Tacos:*
  - 8 small corn tortillas, warmed
  - 1 cup red cabbage, thinly sliced
  - 1 carrot, julienned
  - 1 avocado, sliced
  - Fresh cilantro leaves for garnish
  - Lime wedges for serving

Instructions:

1. Prepare the Duck:
   - Season the duck breasts with salt and pepper.
   - Place the duck skin-side down in a cold non-stick skillet. Turn heat to medium and cook until the fat is rendered and the skin is crisp and golden, about 6-8 minutes.
   - Flip the duck over and cook for an additional 4-5 minutes for medium-rare, or longer to your desired doneness.
   - Remove from heat, let rest for a few minutes, then slice thinly.

2. Make the Jalapeño Soy Glaze:
   - In a small saucepan, combine soy sauce, honey, rice vinegar, water, chopped jalapeño, garlic, and ginger. Bring to a simmer over medium heat.
   - Stir in the cornstarch slurry and continue to cook, stirring constantly, until the sauce thickens, about 1-2 minutes.
   - Remove from heat and set aside.

Instructions Continued:

3. Assemble the Tacos:

    - Warm the corn tortillas in a dry skillet over medium heat until pliable.

    - Divide the sliced duck among the tortillas.

    - Top each taco with sliced red cabbage, julienned carrot, and slices of avocado.

    - Drizzle with the jalapeño soy glaze.

    - Garnish with fresh cilantro leaves.

4. Serve:

    - Serve the tacos immediately with lime wedges on the side for squeezing over.

Korean Fried Cauliflower with Cajun Miso Butter

Difficulty: Medium

Flavor Profile: This dish combines the crispy texture of Korean-style fried cauliflower with the bold, umami flavors of miso and the spicy notes of Cajun seasoning. It's a perfect fusion appetizer that packs a flavorful punch

This Korean Fried Cauliflower with Cajun Miso Butter merges the best of Korean and Southern flavors, offering an irresistible dish that's perfect for parties, gatherings, or even as a tasty snack.

Tips:

- Batter Consistency: Ensure the batter is neither too thick nor too thin to achieve the best coating for frying. If it's too thick, add a little more water; if too thin, a bit more flour.

- Sauce Adjustments: Adjust the amount of Cajun seasoning according to your spice preference. You can also add a splash of hot sauce for extra heat.

- Serving Suggestions: This Korean Fried Cauliflower can be served as an appetizer with toothpicks for easy eating or as a side dish with a main course.

Ingredients:

- *For the Cauliflower:*

  - 1 large head of cauliflower, cut into florets

  - 1 cup all-purpose flour

  - 1/2 cup cornstarch

  - 1 teaspoon baking powder

  - 1 1/2 cups water, cold

  - Salt to taste

  - Oil for frying

Ingredients Continued:

- For the Cajun Miso Butter Sauce:

  - 1/4 cup miso paste (preferably red miso for a deeper flavor)

  - 1/4 cup unsalted butter

  - 1 tablespoon Cajun seasoning

  - 2 cloves garlic, minced

  - 1 tablespoon honey or maple syrup

  - 1 tablespoon soy sauce

  - 1 tablespoon rice vinegar

  - 1 teaspoon sesame oil

- For Garnish:

  - 2 green onions, thinly sliced

  - 1 tablespoon sesame seeds

  - Fresh cilantro, chopped (optional)

Instructions:

1. Prepare the Cauliflower:

   - In a large bowl, whisk together the flour, cornstarch, baking powder, and salt. Add cold water and whisk until the batter is smooth.

   - Heat oil in a deep fryer or large pot to 350°F (175°C).

   - Dip cauliflower florets into the batter, ensuring each piece is well-coated.

   - Fry the battered cauliflower in batches until golden and crispy, about 3-4 minutes per batch. Drain on paper towels.

2. Make the Cajun Miso Butter Sauce:

   - In a small saucepan, melt the butter over medium heat.

   - Add the miso paste, Cajun seasoning, and minced garlic, and stir until well combined.

   - Mix in the honey, soy sauce, rice vinegar, and sesame oil, stirring continuously until the sauce is smooth and heated through.

3. Toss the Cauliflower:

   - In a large bowl, pour the hot Cajun miso butter sauce over the fried cauliflower. Toss gently to coat all the florets evenly.

4. Serve:

   - Transfer the coated cauliflower to a serving platter.

   - Garnish with sliced green onions, sesame seeds, and chopped cilantro if desired.

   - Serve immediately to enjoy the crispy texture of the cauliflower.

Gochujang Glazed Pecan-Crusted Green Beans

Difficulty: Medium

Flavor Profile: This dish combines the spicy and slightly sweet flavors of gochujang with the crunchy texture of pecan-crusted green beans, resulting in a savory, nutty, and vibrant side dish that adds a creative twist to traditional flavors.

This dish offers a delightful blend of textures and flavors, making it an exciting addition to any meal where traditional meets modern in a delicious fusion.

Tips:

- Green Bean Preparation: Ensure the green beans are dry before breading to help the coating adhere better.
- Oil Temperature: Keep the oil hot enough for frying (around 350°F or 175°C) to ensure the green beans become crispy and are not greasy.
- Serving Suggestions: These gochujang glazed pecan-crusted green beans can be served as a side dish with grilled meats or as a unique appetizer with other dipping sauces.

Ingredients:

- *For the Green Beans:*
  - 1 lb fresh green beans, trimmed
  - 1/2 cup flour
  - 1 teaspoon salt
  - 1/2 teaspoon black pepper
  - 2 eggs, beaten
  - 1 cup pecans, finely chopped

Ingredients Continued:

- Oil for frying

- *For the Gochujang Glaze:*

  - 1/4 cup gochujang (Korean chili paste)
  - 2 tablespoons honey or brown sugar
  - 2 tablespoons soy sauce
  - 1 tablespoon rice vinegar
  - 1 tablespoon sesame oil
  - 1 clove garlic, minced
  - 1 teaspoon ginger, grated

Instructions:

1. Prepare the Green Beans:
    - Blanch the green beans in boiling water for 2-3 minutes until bright green but still crisp. Drain and immediately plunge into ice water to stop the cooking process. Drain again and dry thoroughly.

2. Breading and Frying:
    - Set up a breading station with three shallow dishes: one for flour mixed with salt and pepper, one for beaten eggs, and one for finely chopped pecans.
    - Dredge the green beans first in the seasoned flour, then dip into the beaten eggs, and finally coat thoroughly with the chopped pecans.
    - Heat oil in a frying pan over medium heat. Fry the coated green beans in batches until golden brown and crispy, about 2-3 minutes per side. Drain on paper towels.

3. Make the Gochujang Glaze:
    - In a small saucepan, combine the gochujang, honey (or brown sugar), soy sauce, rice vinegar, sesame oil, minced garlic, and grated ginger.
    - Heat over medium-low, stirring constantly until the ingredients are well combined and the mixture is smooth and heated through.

4. Finish and Serve:
    - Drizzle the gochujang glaze over the fried green beans or serve it on the side for dipping.
    - Optionally, sprinkle with additional chopped pecans or sesame seeds for garnish.

Bacon Mochi Sticks

Difficulty: Advanced

Flavor Profile: These unique appetizers blend the savory, smoky flavor of bacon with the chewy, slightly sweet texture of mochi, creating an intriguing fusion snack that's both satisfying and memorable.

Bacon Mochi Sticks offer a delightful contrast in textures and flavors, making them a sure hit for those who enjoy adventurous eating and fusion cuisine.

Tips:
- Microwave Power Variance: Cooking times may vary based on your microwave's power, so adjust the cooking time accordingly.
- Handling Mochi: Mochi is very sticky; using mochiko for dusting hands and surfaces helps manage this.
- Serving Suggestions: These sticks make a great party snack or a side dish to a larger meal. They combine well with other Asian-inspired dishes for a themed dinner night.

Ingredients:
- *For the Mochi:*
  - 1 cup mochiko (sweet rice flour)
  - 1/4 cup sugar
  - 1/2 teaspoon baking powder
  - 1 cup water

Ingredients Continued:

- 1/2 teaspoon vanilla extract (optional)

- *Additional Ingredients:*

- 10-12 slices of bacon, thin to medium thickness

- Oil for frying (if needed)

- *For Serving:*

- Soy sauce for dipping

- Optional: a drizzle of honey or maple syrup

- Optional: sprinkle of sesame seeds or chopped green onions for garnish

Instructions:

1. Prepare the Mochi Dough:

   - In a mixing bowl, combine mochiko, sugar, and baking powder. Mix thoroughly to distribute the ingredients evenly.

   - Add water and vanilla extract to the dry ingredients. Stir until well combined and a thick batter forms. It should be pourable but thick.

2. Cook the Mochi:

   - Pour the mochi batter into a greased microwave-safe dish. Smooth the top with a spatula.

   - Microwave on high for about 7-10 minutes, or until the mochi is set and slightly translucent.

   - Remove from the microwave and let cool slightly until it can be handled.

3. Form Mochi Sticks:

   - Once the mochi is cool enough to handle, turn it out onto a surface dusted with more mochiko to prevent sticking.

   - Cut the mochi into strips about 1 inch wide and 4 inches long. Dust your hands and the mochi with mochiko as needed to prevent sticking.

4. Wrap with Bacon:

   - Wrap each mochi stick with a slice of bacon, securing the ends with toothpicks if necessary.

5. Cook the Bacon Mochi Sticks:

   - Preheat your oven to 400°F (200°C) or prepare to fry.

   - For Baking: Place the bacon-wrapped mochi on a baking sheet lined with parchment paper. Bake in the preheated oven for 20-25 minutes, turning once, until the bacon is crispy.

   - For Frying: Heat oil in a skillet over medium heat. Fry the bacon-wrapped mochi, turning, occasionally until the bacon is crispy on all sides.

Instructions Continued:

6. Serve:
   - Remove the bacon mochi sticks from the oven or skillet and let them cool slightly on a paper towel-lined plate to absorb excess grease.
   - Serve warm with soy sauce for dipping. Optionally, drizzle with honey or maple syrup and sprinkle with sesame seeds or chopped green onions.

Southern BBQ-Style Char Siu Pork Recipe

Difficulty: Medium

Flavor Profile: A delightful fusion of the sweet and savory richness of traditional Chinese Char Siu with the smoky depth of Southern barbecue.

This dish bridges Eastern and Western culinary traditions, offering a perfect blend for a festive gathering or a family dinner.

Tips:

- Marinade Penetration: To ensure the marinade penetrates deeply, occasionally massage the marinade into the meat through the bag during the marination process.
- Monitoring Grill Temperature: Keep a close eye on the grill temperature to avoid burning the marinade, which can happen due to its sugar content.

Ingredients:

- *Main Components:*
  - 2 lbs pork tenderloin or pork belly

- *For the Marinade:*
  - 1/4 cup hoisin sauce
  - 1/4 cup Southern barbecue sauce (preferably a smoky variety)
  - 2 tablespoons soy sauce
  - 2 tablespoons honey
  - 2 tablespoons brown sugar
  - 2 cloves garlic, minced
  - 1 tablespoon Chinese five-spice powder
  - 1 teaspoon smoked paprika
  - 1 tablespoon rice vinegar
  - 1 teaspoon sesame oil
  - Optional: Red food coloring for traditional Char Siu color

- *Seasonings:*
  - Salt and black pepper to taste

- *For Garnish:*
  - Sesame seeds
  - Sliced green onions

Instructions:

1. Prepare the Marinade:
    - In a mixing bowl, whisk together hoisin sauce, barbecue sauce, soy sauce, honey, brown sugar, minced garlic, Chinese five-spice powder, smoked paprika, rice vinegar, and sesame oil until well combined.
    - Optionally, add a few drops of red food coloring to achieve the characteristic red hue of traditional Char Siu.

2. Marinate the Pork:
    - Trim any excess fat from the pork and cut it into long strips approximately 2 inches thick. Season lightly with salt and black pepper.
    - Place the pork strips in a large resealable plastic bag or a shallow dish. Pour the marinade over the pork, ensuring all pieces are thoroughly coated.
    - Seal the bag or cover the dish and refrigerate for at least 4 hours, though overnight marination is preferable for deeper flavor penetration.

3. Prepare for Cooking:
    - Remove the pork from the refrigerator at least 30 minutes before cooking to bring it to room temperature, ensuring more even cooking.

4. Cook the Pork:
    - *Grilling Method:*
       - Preheat your grill to medium-high heat.
       - Place the pork strips on the grill and cook for 10-12 minutes on each side, basting frequently with the leftover marinade, until the outside is nicely caramelized and the internal temperature reaches 145°F (63°C).
    - *Roasting Method:*
       - Preheat your oven to 350°F (175°C).
       - Place the pork strips on a rack in a roasting pan and roast for about 25-30 minutes, basting occasionally with the marinade, until the pork is caramelized and cooked through.

5. Rest and Serve:
    - Allow the cooked pork to rest for 10 minutes after cooking. This resting period helps the juices redistribute throughout the meat, enhancing its juiciness and flavor.
    - Slice the pork into bite-sized pieces.
    - Garnish with sesame seeds and sliced green onions.
    - Serve hot. This dish pairs excellently with steamed rice, stir-fried vegetables, or can be used as a delicious filling for buns and sandwiches.

BBQ Pork Stuffed Buttermilk Biscuits

Difficulty: Medium

Flavor Profile: Rich, savory pork with sweet Chinese BBQ flavors, encased in a buttery, flaky buttermilk biscuit.

These biscuits combine the comfort of Southern baking with the sweet and savory flavors of Chinese BBQ pork, creating a handheld delight that's perfect for any time of day.

Ingredients:
- 2 cups all-purpose flour
- 1 tbsp baking powder
- 1/2 tsp baking soda
- 1 tsp salt
- 1/2 cup unsalted butter, cold and cubed
- 3/4 cup buttermilk
- 1/2 lb Chinese BBQ pork (char siu), finely chopped

Ingredients Continued:

Ginger-Scallion Gravy:

- 2 tbsp unsalted butter
- 2 tbsp all-purpose flour
- 2 cups chicken broth
- 1 tbsp soy sauce
- 2 tbsp finely chopped scallions
- 1 tsp minced ginger

Instructions:

1. Prepare the Biscuits:
    - Preheat the oven to 425°F (220°C).
    - In a large bowl, whisk together the flour, baking powder, baking soda, and salt.
    - Cut in the cold butter using a pastry cutter or your fingers until the mixture resembles coarse crumbs.

2. Make the Dough:
    - Stir in the buttermilk until just combined.
    - Turn the dough out onto a floured surface and gently knead a few times.
    - Roll out to 1/2-inch thickness.

3. Fill the Biscuits:
    - Cut out biscuits using a 3-inch round cutter.
    - Place a spoonful of chopped BBQ pork in the center of half the biscuits.
    - Top with another biscuit round and press the edges to seal.

4. Bake the Biscuits:
    - Place the biscuits on a baking sheet and bake for 12-15 minutes, until golden brown.

5. Make the Gravy:
    - In a small saucepan, melt the butter over medium heat.
    - Stir in the flour and cook for 1 minute.
    - Gradually whisk in the chicken broth, soy sauce, scallions, and ginger.
    - Simmer until thickened, about 5 minutes.

6. Serve:
    - Serve the biscuits warm, drizzled with ginger-scallion gravy.

BBQ Pork Bao Sliders

Difficulty: Easy

Flavor Profile: Rich, savory pork with sweet, tangy hoisin-bourbon glaze, balanced by the freshness of pickled onions and cucumbers.

These sliders combine the soft, pillowy texture of bao buns with the richness of BBQ pork, bringing together the best of both worlds.

Ingredients:
- 1 lb Chinese BBQ pork (char siu)
- 1 tbsp salt
- 1 tbsp sugar
- 12 small bao buns (store-bought or homemade)
- 1 cucumber, thinly sliced
- 1/2 cup pickled red onions

Hoisin-Bourbon Glaze:
- 1/4 cup hoisin sauce
- 2 tbsp bourbon
- 1 tbsp soy sauce
- 1 tbsp honey
- 1 tsp sesame oil
- 1 clove garlic, minced

Instructions:
1. Make the Glaze:
   - In a small saucepan, combine hoisin sauce, bourbon, soy sauce, honey, sesame oil, and minced garlic.
   - Simmer over low heat for 5 minutes, until slightly thickened.

2. Assemble the Sliders:
   - Open the bao buns and fill each with a slice of pork belly, a few cucumber slices, and pickled red onions.
   - Drizzle with hoisin-bourbon glaze.

3. Serve:
   - Serve the sliders warm, garnished with fresh cilantro if desired.

Pickling Guide

Combining Southern and Asian flavors in pickles offers a unique twist on traditional pickling recipes. Here are 10 recipes and tips for creating vibrant, flavorful pickles that blend the tangy, sweet, and spicy flavors characteristic of both cuisines.

You can incorporate these pickles into various recipes

1. Spicy Bourbon Pickled Jalapeños
    - Combine sliced jalapeños, bourbon, white vinegar, sugar, and garlic. Let sit for at least 48 hours before using.

2. Sweet Tea Cucumber Pickles
    - Steep cucumbers in a brine of sweet tea, apple cider vinegar, and spices like cloves and cinnamon for a Southern twist.

3. Ginger Pickled Carrots
    - Slice carrots and pickle them in a mixture of rice vinegar, water, sugar, salt, and fresh ginger slices for a zesty side dish.

4. Szechuan Peppercorn Pickled Green Beans
    - Quick-pickle green beans in a brine of Szechuan peppercorns, soy sauce, rice vinegar, and a dash of sesame oil.

5. Kimchi-Spiced Okra
    - Ferment okra with kimchi brine, garlic, and Korean chili flakes for a spicy, crunchy snack.

6. Miso-Maple Pickled Eggs
    - Hard-boil eggs and pickle them in a mixture of miso paste, maple syrup, and water for a unique protein-rich snack.

7. Honey-Sriracha Pickled Radish
    - Slice radishes and pickle them in a brine of honey, Sriracha, rice vinegar, and salt for a hot and sweet treat.

8. Lemongrass Pickled Shrimp
    - Marinate cooked shrimp in a lemongrass-infused vinegar solution with garlic and chili peppers for a light, flavorful appetizer.

9. Five-Spice Pickled Peaches
   - Pit and quarter peaches, then pickle them in a brine seasoned with Chinese five-spice, sugar, and white vinegar.

10. Garlic-Dill Pickled Watermelon Rinds
    - Use watermelon rinds in a dill and garlic brine for a Southern-inspired twist on a classic pickle recipe.

Tips for Successful Pickling

- Use Fresh Ingredients: Always start with fresh, clean produce for the best flavor and texture.
- Keep Everything Clean: Ensure all jars and utensils are sterilized to prevent contamination.
- Balance Flavors: Adjust the sweetness, acidity, and saltiness to suit your taste. Experiment with different spices to find your perfect combination.
- Monitor the Pickles: Keep an eye on your pickles as they ferment. Taste them at various stages to achieve your desired flavor profile.
- Store Properly: Keep pickles refrigerated after opening to maintain their crispness and prevent spoilage.

SOUPS
SANDWICHES
& SALADS

Tom Yum Gumbo

Difficulty: Medium

Flavor Profile: This dish is a fusion of Louisiana-style gumbo and Thai Tom Yum soup, combining the rich, hearty flavors of shrimp, sausage, and mushrooms with the bright, citrusy, and tangy notes of Tom Yum. It's spicy, savory, and full of vibrant flavors.

This recipe combines the comforting, soul-warming qualities of gumbo with the bold, zesty flavors of Tom Yum, making it a unique fusion dish perfect for anyone who loves both Southern and Thai cuisine.

Tips:

- Okra Consistency: If you prefer a thicker gumbo, let the okra cook a little longer to release its natural thickening agents. For a thinner consistency, cook the okra for less time.
- Kaffir Lime Leaves: If you can find kaffir lime leaves, they add an authentic Tom Yum flavor to the broth. Crush the leaves gently before adding them to the pot to release their oils.
- Seafood Alternatives: Feel free to substitute or add other types of seafood like crab or clams for a richer, more varied seafood gumbo.
- Serving Suggestions: Serve the gumbo with a side of crusty bread or cornbread to soak up the flavorful broth.

Ingredients:

- *For the Gumbo:*
  - 1/2 lb shrimp, peeled and deveined
  - 1/2 lb andouille sausage, sliced
  - 1 onion, chopped
  - 1 bell pepper, chopped
  - 2 stalks celery, chopped
  - 4 cloves garlic, minced
  - 1 tablespoon red curry paste
  - 6 cups chicken broth
  - 1 can coconut milk (13.5 oz)
  - 1 tablespoon fish sauce
  - 1 tablespoon lime juice
  - 2 cups fresh okra, sliced into 1/2 inch rounds
  - 8 oz mushrooms, sliced (shiitake or button mushrooms work well)
  - 2 tablespoons lemongrass, minced (optional for extra Tom Yum flavor)
  - 3-4 kaffir lime leaves (optional)
  - Jasmine rice for serving
  - Fresh cilantro, chopped, for garnish
  - Lime wedges for serving

Instructions:

1. Sauté the Vegetables:
    - Heat a tablespoon of oil in a large pot over medium heat. Add the chopped onion, bell pepper, and celery (the "holy trinity" of gumbo) and sauté until softened and fragrant, about 5-7 minutes.
    - Add the minced garlic, lemongrass (if using), and red curry paste. Stir and cook for an additional 2 minutes until the spices are fragrant.

2. Add the Sausage and Broth:
    - Stir in the sliced andouille sausage and cook for 3-4 minutes until slightly browned.
    - Pour in the chicken broth and coconut milk, stirring to combine. Add the kaffir lime leaves if using. Bring the mixture to a gentle boil, then reduce the heat and let it simmer for 10-15 minutes to allow the flavors to meld.

3. Add the Seafood and Vegetables:
    - Add the shrimp, sliced okra, and mushrooms to the pot. Simmer for an additional 5-7 minutes until the shrimp turn pink and are cooked through. The okra will naturally thicken the broth, giving the gumbo its signature texture.

Instructions Continued:

4. Finish the Gumbo:
   - Stir in the fish sauce and lime juice to bring a bright, tangy finish to the dish. Taste and adjust the seasoning with salt and pepper as needed.
   - If you want a little extra heat, you can stir in some crushed red pepper flakes or Thai chili paste at this point.

5. Serve:
   - Serve the Tom Yum Gumbo over jasmine rice. Garnish with fresh cilantro and a squeeze of lime juice for extra brightness.

6. Optional Garnishes:
   - Additional toppings like crispy fried shallots, toasted coconut flakes, or even a drizzle of sriracha can add more depth to the dish.

Pho with Smoked Brisket

Difficulty: Medium

Flavor Profile: This recipe marries the deep, aromatic essence of traditional Vietnamese pho with the rich, smoky flavors of Southern-style smoked brisket, creating a comforting and satisfying fusion dish.

This Pho with Smoked Brisket recipe brings an innovative twist to the traditional Vietnamese dish, integrating the smoky, deep flavors of Southern barbecue into the complex, spiced broth of pho, creating a cross-cultural culinary experience that's both hearty and soul-warming.

Tips:

- Broth Flavoring: For best results, toast the spices for the broth before adding them to the pot to enhance their flavors.
- Noodle Preparation: Ensure not to overcook the noodles – they should be just tender as they will continue to soften when hot broth is poured over them.
- Serving: This dish is best served hot and fresh. The garnishes are crucial as they add fresh, contrasting flavors that balance the rich, spiced broth and smoky meat.

Ingredients:

- *For the Smoked Brisket:*

  - 2 lbs beef brisket

  - 2 tablespoons salt

  - 1 tablespoon black pepper

  - 1 tablespoon smoked paprika

- *For the Pho Broth:*

  - 2 onions, halved

  - 4-inch piece of ginger, halved lengthwise

  - 3 quarts beef broth

  - 2 star anise

  - 2 cinnamon sticks

  - 4 cloves

  - 1 cardamom pod

  - 1 teaspoon fennel seeds

  - 1 teaspoon coriander seeds

  - 1/4 cup fish sauce

  - 1 tablespoon sugar

- *For the Pho Assembly:*

  - 1 lb rice noodles, prepared according to package instructions

  - 2 cups bean sprouts

  - 1 bunch cilantro, roughly chopped

  - 1 bunch green onions, thinly sliced

  - 1 lime, cut into wedges

  - 2 jalapeños, thinly sliced

  - Fresh basil leaves

  - Hoisin sauce

  - Sriracha sauce

Instructions:

1. Prepare the Brisket:

   - Season the brisket with salt, pepper, and smoked paprika.

   - Smoke the brisket in a smoker set to 225°F (107°C) for about 6 to 8 hours, or until the internal temperature reaches 190°F (88°C). Once done, let it rest, then slice thinly against the grain.

Instructions Continued:

2. Char the Onions and Ginger:
    - Char the halved onions and ginger under a broiler or over an open flame until they are slightly blackened. This adds depth to the broth.

3. Prepare the Pho Broth:
    - In a large pot, add the beef broth along with the charred onions and ginger, star anise, cinnamon sticks, cloves, cardamom, fennel seeds, and coriander seeds.
    - Bring to a boil, then reduce to a simmer for about 1 to 1.5 hours to allow the flavors to meld.
    - Strain the broth, removing the spices and aromatics. Return the broth to the pot.
    - Season the broth with fish sauce and sugar, adjusting to taste.

4. Assemble the Pho:
    - Arrange cooked rice noodles in bowls.
    - Add slices of the smoked brisket to each bowl.
    - Ladle the hot broth over the noodles and brisket, making sure to cover them well to heat the meat thoroughly.

5. Garnish and Serve:
    - Serve the pho with plates of bean sprouts, chopped cilantro, sliced green onions, lime wedges, sliced jalapeños, and basil leaves on the side.
    - Allow guests to add hoisin sauce and sriracha to their liking.

Peanut Chicken and Sweet Potato Dumplings

Difficulty: High

Flavor Profile: A hearty and comforting dish featuring succulent chicken in a savory peanut broth, complemented by uniquely flavored sweet potato dumplings.

This Chicken and Dumplings with Peanut Broth and Sweet Potato Dumplings recipe is a delightful twist on a classic comfort food, introducing the nutty richness of peanut and the sweet, earthy flavor of sweet potatoes into the traditional dish.

Tips:
- Sweet Potato Consistency: Ensure the sweet potato is finely grated to blend easily into the dumpling dough.
- Broth Thickness: If the broth is too thick after adding the peanut butter, add more chicken broth or water to reach your desired consistency.
- Serving Suggestion: This dish is hearty on its own but can be paired with a simple green salad or steamed vegetables for a complete meal.

Ingredients:

- *For the Peanut Broth:*
  - 2 tablespoons olive oil
  - 1 large onion, finely chopped
  - 2 cloves garlic, minced
  - 1 tablespoon grated ginger
  - 6 cups chicken broth
  - 1 cup creamy peanut butter
  - 2 tablespoons soy sauce
  - 1 teaspoon chili flakes (optional for heat)
  - Salt and pepper to taste

- *For the Chicken:*
  - 2 lbs chicken thighs, boneless and skinless, cut into bite-sized pieces

- *For the Sweet Potato Dumplings:*
  - 1 large sweet potato, peeled and grated
  - 2 cups all-purpose flour
  - 1 teaspoon baking powder
  - 1/2 teaspoon salt
  - 3/4 cup milk

- *Additional Ingredients:*
  - Fresh cilantro, chopped for garnish
  - Chopped peanuts, for garnish

Instructions:

1. Prepare the Peanut Broth:
   - In a large pot, heat the olive oil over medium heat. Add the onion and sauté until translucent, about 5 minutes.
   - Add the minced garlic and grated ginger, cooking for another 2 minutes until fragrant.
   - Pour in the chicken broth and bring to a simmer.
   - Stir in the peanut butter, soy sauce, and chili flakes (if using). Reduce heat and continue to simmer gently, stirring occasionally to ensure the peanut butter is fully integrated into the broth. Season with salt and pepper.

Instructions Continued:

2. Cook the Chicken:
   - Add the chicken pieces to the simmering broth. Cook over medium heat until the chicken is thoroughly cooked, about 15-20 minutes.

3. Make the Sweet Potato Dumplings:
   - In a mixing bowl, combine the grated sweet potato, flour, baking powder, and salt. Gradually add the milk to form a sticky dough.
   - Once the chicken is cooked, drop tablespoon-sized dollops of the dumpling dough directly into the simmering broth. Cover the pot and let the dumplings cook until they rise to the surface and are cooked through, about 15 minutes.

4. Final Adjustments and Serve:
   - Taste the broth and adjust seasoning if necessary.
   - Ladle the chicken, dumplings, and broth into bowls.
   - Garnish with chopped cilantro and peanuts before serving.

Sweet Potato and Ginger Congee

Difficulty: Easy

Flavor Profile: A warming, comforting porridge with the earthy sweetness of sweet potatoes and the spicy kick of fresh ginger, providing a soothing, nourishing meal perfect for chilly days or when you need a gentle dish.

This Sweet Potato and Ginger Congee is a delightful fusion of Southern comfort ingredients and traditional Asian-style rice porridge, offering a comforting meal that's both nutritious and easy to digest. Perfect for breakfast, a light lunch, or a soothing dinner.

Tips:
- Congee Consistency: Congee can be made as thick or as thin as you like. Simply adjust the amount of broth during cooking to achieve your preferred consistency.
- Cooking Time: The longer the congee cooks, the softer and more broken down the rice will become, enhancing the creamy texture.
- Additional Proteins: For a more substantial meal, consider adding cooked, shredded chicken, diced tofu, or even a softly poached egg on top of each serving.
- Sweet Potato Note: Grating the sweet potato helps it to cook quickly and integrate smoothly into the congee, but you can also dice it if you prefer more texture.

Ingredients:

- *For the Congee*:
  - 1 cup jasmine or short-grain rice
  - 6-8 cups chicken or vegetable broth (adjust based on desired thickness)
  - 1 large sweet potato, peeled and grated
  - 2 inches fresh ginger, peeled and finely grated
  - 1 teaspoon salt, or to taste

- *Garnish and Additional Flavorings:*
  - 2 green onions, thinly sliced
  - 1 small bunch cilantro, chopped
  - Soy sauce, for seasoning
  - Sesame oil, for drizzling
  - A pinch of white pepper
  - Roasted peanuts or cashews, crushed (optional)
  - Fried garlic or shallots (optional)

Instructions:

1. Prepare the Rice:
   - Rinse the rice under cold water until the water runs clear. This helps to remove excess starch and prevent the congee from becoming too gluey.

2. Cook the Congee:
   - In a large pot, combine the rinsed rice and 6 cups of broth. Bring to a boil over high heat.
   - Once boiling, reduce the heat to low, allowing the mixture to simmer gently. Stir occasionally to prevent the rice from sticking to the bottom of the pot.

3. Add Sweet Potatoes and Ginger:
   - After the rice has been simmering for about 20 minutes and is beginning to break down, add the grated sweet potato and ginger to the pot.
   - Continue to cook, stirring frequently, until the congee is thick and creamy, and the rice grains are mostly broken down, about 30 more minutes. Add more broth if the congee is too thick or if a thinner consistency is desired.

4. Season the Congee:
   - Stir in the salt, and adjust the seasoning to your taste. If desired, add a dash of soy sauce for depth of flavor and a pinch of white pepper for slight heat.

Instructions Continued:

5. Serve:
   - Ladle the hot congee into bowls.
   - Garnish each serving with sliced green onions, chopped cilantro, a drizzle of sesame oil, and optionally, roasted nuts, fried garlic, or shallots.
   - Serve immediately, allowing each diner to add additional soy sauce or sesame oil to their liking.

Teriyaki Brunswick Stew

Difficulty: Medium

Flavor Profile: This fusion dish combines the classic, hearty elements of Southern Brunswick stew with the sweet and savory flavors of Japanese teriyaki, creating a unique and delicious comfort food experience.

This Teriyaki Brunswick Stew is a delightful twist on traditional Southern cooking, introducing a touch of Japanese flavor that transforms it into an intriguing fusion dish ideal for cold days or whenever you crave a comforting, filling meal.

Tips:
- Adjusting Flavor: You can adjust the amount of teriyaki sauce used according to your taste preference. Add more for a sweeter, stronger flavor or less for a subtler effect.
- Meat Choices: This stew traditionally uses a mix of meats. Feel free to include smoked sausage or leftover barbecued meats to add depth to the flavor profile.
- Cooking Time: Brunswick stew is known for its thick, rich consistency, which develops better the longer it simmers. If time allows, let it cook longer on a low heat to enhance the flavors even more.

Ingredients:
- *For the Teriyaki Sauce*:
  - 1/2 cup soy sauce
  - 1/4 cup water
  - 2 tablespoons mirin (Japanese rice wine)
  - 1/4 cup brown sugar
  - 2 cloves garlic, minced
  - 1 inch fresh ginger, grated
  - 2 tablespoons cornstarch dissolved in 2 tablespoons water

- *For the Stew:*
  - 2 tablespoons vegetable oil
  - 1 lb chicken thighs, cut into bite-sized pieces
  - 1 lb pork shoulder, cut into bite-sized pieces
  - 1 large onion, chopped
  - 2 cloves garlic, minced
  - 1 cup frozen lima beans
  - 1 cup frozen corn kernels
  - 2 large potatoes, peeled and diced
  - 1 can (28 oz) crushed tomatoes
  - 3 cups chicken broth
  - 1/2 cup prepared teriyaki sauce (from above)
  - Salt and pepper to taste
  - local vegetables, chopped (optional)

- *Garnish*:
  - Chopped green onions
  - Sesame seeds

Instructions:
1. Make the Teriyaki Sauce:
   - In a small saucepan, combine soy sauce, water, mirin, brown sugar, minced garlic, and grated ginger. Bring to a simmer over medium heat.
   - Stir in the cornstarch slurry and continue to cook, stirring constantly, until the sauce thickens, about 1-2 minutes. Remove from heat and set aside.

Instructions Continued:

2. Brown the Meats:
   - In a large pot or Dutch oven, heat vegetable oil over medium-high heat.
   - Add chicken and pork pieces in batches, browning them on all sides. Remove the browned meat and set aside.

3. Sauté the Vegetables:
   - In the same pot, add chopped onion and minced garlic. Sauté until the onions become translucent.
   - Return the browned meat to the pot along with the lima beans, corn, and diced potatoes. Stir to combine.
   - Feel free to sauté and add in other locally available vegetables

4. Simmer the Stew:
   - Add the crushed tomatoes and chicken broth to the pot. Bring the mixture to a boil, then reduce to a simmer.
   - Stir in 1/2 cup of the prepared teriyaki sauce. Season with salt and pepper.
   - Cover and let simmer for about 1-1.5 hours, or until the meat is tender and the flavors have melded together.

5. Finish and Serve:
   - Taste the stew and adjust seasoning if needed. If the stew is too thick, add more chicken broth or water to reach the desired consistency.
   - Serve hot, garnished with chopped green onions and a sprinkle of sesame seeds.

Jalapeño and Pork Belly Miso Soup

Difficulty: Medium

Flavor Profile: This soup combines the rich, savory depth of pork belly with the umami richness of miso and a spicy kick from jalapeños, creating a comforting and flavorful fusion dish perfect for cooler weather or whenever you need a warming meal.

This Jalapeño and Pork Belly Miso Soup is a sumptuous fusion that brings together Japanese and Southern elements for a truly unique culinary experience, offering both comfort and a satisfying complexity of flavors.

Tips:

- Adjusting Soup Thickness: If you prefer a thicker soup, you can dissolve an additional tablespoon of miso paste in a little broth and add it to the pot.
- Handling Miso: Always add miso at the end of cooking to preserve its flavor and health benefits, as high heat can destroy some of its properties.
- Variations: For an even more robust flavor, consider adding a splash of sake to the broth during cooking, or garnish with nori strips for an extra umami kick.

Ingredients:
- *For the Pork Belly:*
  - 1 lb pork belly, cut into 1-inch cubes
  - Salt and pepper, to taste

- *For the Soup Base:*
  - 4 cups dashi broth (or substitute with chicken or vegetable broth)
  - 1/4 cup white miso paste
  - 2 tablespoons soy sauce
  - 1 tablespoon mirin
  - 1-2 jalapeños, thinly sliced (adjust based on heat preference)
  - 2 cloves garlic, minced
  - 1 inch piece of ginger, peeled and grated

- *Additional Ingredients:*
  - 1 cup tofu, diced
  - 1 cup shiitake mushrooms, sliced
  - 2 green onions, sliced
  - 1 cup spinach or kale, roughly chopped
  - Optional: 1 teaspoon sesame oil for drizzling

Instructions:
1. Prepare the Pork Belly:
   - Season the pork belly cubes with salt and pepper.
   - In a large pot or skillet, render the pork belly over medium heat until it is golden and crisp on all sides. This process may take about 10-15 minutes.
   - Remove the pork belly from the pot and set aside on a paper towel-lined plate to drain excess fat.

2. Prepare the Soup Base:
   - In the same pot used for the pork belly, remove all but one tablespoon of the rendered fat. Add garlic and ginger, and sauté until fragrant, about 1 minute.
   - Pour in the dashi broth. Bring to a simmer over medium heat.
   - In a small bowl, mix the miso paste with a little hot broth until smooth, then stir back into the pot to avoid lumps.
   - Add soy sauce, mirin, and sliced jalapeños to the broth, adjusting the jalapeños depending on your heat preference.

Instructions Continued:

3. Simmer the Ingredients:
    -   Return the crisped pork belly to the pot.
    -   Add shiitake mushrooms and tofu. Let the soup simmer gently for about 10 minutes to allow the flavors to meld and the tofu to absorb the soup flavors.

4. Finish the Soup:
    -   Just before serving, add the sliced green onions and chopped spinach or kale to the soup. Allow the greens to wilt slightly, which should take about 2-3 minutes.
    -   If desired, drizzle a teaspoon of sesame oil over the soup for added flavor.

5. Serve:
    -   Ladle the soup into bowls, making sure to distribute pork belly, tofu, and vegetables evenly.
    -   Serve hot, perhaps with a side of steamed rice or extra slices of jalapeño for those who appreciate more heat.

Sake Braised Chicken and Rice Soup

Difficulty: Medium

Flavor Profile: This comforting soup blends the subtle, aromatic flavors of sake with the richness of braised chicken, complemented by hearty rice, making it a perfect fusion of Japanese and Southern culinary traditions.

This Sake Braised Chicken and Rice Soup offers a delightful fusion that is both nourishing and rich in flavor, ideal for chilly evenings or when you need a comforting meal that soothes and satisfies.

Tips:

- Choosing Sake: Use a good-quality sake that you enjoy drinking, as the flavor will concentrate as it cooks.
- Rice Considerations: Be mindful that rice continues to absorb liquid as it sits, so if you have leftovers, you may need to add more broth when reheating.
- Serving Suggestion: This soup is hearty enough to serve as a main course but can also be paired with a simple salad or steamed vegetables for a fuller meal.

Ingredients:

- *For the Chicken*:
  - 1 lb chicken thighs, bone-in and skin-on
  - Salt and pepper, to taste
  - 2 tablespoons vegetable oil

- *For the Soup*:
  - 1 onion, diced
  - 2 carrots, peeled and diced
  - 2 celery stalks, diced
  - 3 cloves garlic, minced
  - 1 inch piece of ginger, peeled and minced
  - 1/2 cup sake
  - 4 cups chicken broth
  - 1 cup water
  - 1/2 cup short-grain rice or jasmine rice
  - 1 tablespoon soy sauce
  - 1 tablespoon mirin
  - 2 teaspoons sesame oil
  - 1 bay leaf

- *Additional Ingredients*:
  - 2 green onions, thinly sliced
  - Fresh cilantro or parsley, chopped for garnish
  - Optional: lemon wedges for serving

Instructions:

1. Prepare the Chicken:
   - Season the chicken thighs generously with salt and pepper.
   - Heat vegetable oil in a large pot over medium-high heat. Once hot, add the chicken, skin-side down, and sear until golden brown, about 3-4 minutes per side. Remove the chicken from the pot and set aside.

2. Sauté the Vegetables:
   - In the same pot, reduce the heat to medium. Add the diced onion, carrots, and celery. Cook, stirring occasionally, until the vegetables begin to soften, about 5 minutes.
   - Add the minced garlic and ginger, cooking for another 1-2 minutes until fragrant.

Instructions Continued:

3. Deglaze with Sake:
    - Pour in the sake to deglaze the pot, scraping up any browned bits from the bottom. Allow the sake to reduce by half, which will take about 3-4 minutes.

4. Simmer the Soup:
    - Return the chicken thighs to the pot. Add chicken broth, water, soy sauce, mirin, sesame oil, and a bay leaf.
    - Bring the mixture to a boil, then reduce to a simmer. Cover and let it cook for 25 minutes.

5. Add Rice:
    - After the chicken has been simmering for 25 minutes, add the rice to the pot. Continue to simmer, covered, for an additional 20 minutes, or until the rice is fully cooked and the chicken is tender.

6. Final Preparations:
    - Remove the chicken thighs from the soup. Discard the skin and bones, and shred the meat using two forks.
    - Return the shredded chicken to the pot. Stir well to distribute the chicken throughout the soup.

7. Serve:
    - Taste and adjust seasoning with additional soy sauce or salt if necessary.
    - Ladle the soup into bowls, and garnish with sliced green onions and chopped cilantro or parsley.
    - Serve with lemon wedges on the side if desired.

Thai Basil and Tomato Soup with Kimchi Grilled Cheese

Difficulty: Medium

Flavor Profile: This vibrant and aromatic soup pairs the fresh, peppery flavor of Thai basil with the tangy richness of tomato, accompanied by a spicy and tangy kimchi grilled cheese sandwich for a perfect fusion of Asian and Southern flavors.

This Thai Basil and Tomato Soup with Kimchi Grilled Cheese combines the comforting familiarity of tomato soup and grilled cheese with exciting new flavors, making it a perfect meal for those looking to spice up their culinary routine.

Tips:

- Tomato Selection: For the best flavor, use ripe, in-season tomatoes. In the off-season, canned tomatoes can provide a richer taste.
- Soup Consistency: If the soup is too thick after blending, adjust by adding a bit more vegetable broth or water until desired consistency is achieved.
- Cheese Choice: Cheddar cheese works well with kimchi due to its sharpness, but feel free to experiment with other types like mozzarella or Gouda for different melting properties and flavors.

Ingredients:

- *For the Thai Basil and Tomato Soup:*
  - 2 tablespoons olive oil
  - 1 onion, finely chopped
  - 3 cloves garlic, minced
  - 1-inch piece ginger, grated
  - 1 red chili, deseeded and finely chopped (optional)
  - 2 pounds ripe tomatoes, chopped (or 2 cans of diced tomatoes)
  - 4 cups vegetable broth
  - 1/4 cup fresh Thai basil, chopped
  - 1 teaspoon sugar
  - Salt and pepper to taste
  - 1 can (14 oz) coconut milk

- *For the Kimchi Grilled Cheese:*
  - 8 slices sourdough bread
  - 1 cup kimchi, drained and chopped
  - 2 cups grated cheddar cheese
  - Butter for spreading

Instructions:

1. Make the Thai Basil and Tomato Soup:
   - Heat the olive oil in a large pot over medium heat. Add the chopped onion and sauté until translucent, about 5 minutes.
   - Add the minced garlic, grated ginger, and red chili (if using) to the pot and sauté for another 2 minutes until fragrant.
   - Stir in the chopped tomatoes and cook for about 10 minutes, until the tomatoes are broken down and saucy.
   - Pour in the vegetable broth and bring the mixture to a boil. Reduce heat and let it simmer for 20 minutes.
   - Remove from heat and stir in the chopped Thai basil, sugar, and season with salt and pepper.
   - Use an immersion blender to blend the soup until smooth. Stir in the coconut milk and return the pot to low heat, warming the soup through without letting it boil.
   - Taste and adjust seasoning if necessary.

Instructions Continued:

2. Prepare the Kimchi Grilled Cheese:
   - Butter one side of each slice of sourdough bread.
   - On the non-buttered side of four slices, evenly distribute half of the grated cheese.
   - Top the cheese with chopped kimchi, then sprinkle the remaining cheese over the kimchi.
   - Cover with the remaining slices of bread, buttered side up.
   - Heat a skillet over medium heat. Once hot, place the sandwiches in the skillet, pressing them lightly with a spatula.
   - Cook until the bread is golden brown and the cheese is melted, about 3-4 minutes per side.

3. Serve:
   - Ladle the warm Thai basil and tomato soup into bowls.
   - Cut the kimchi grilled cheese sandwiches in half and serve alongside the soup for dipping.

Honey Almond Shrimp Po'Boy Sandwich

Difficulty: Medium

Flavor Profile: A delightful blend of sweet, nutty, and savory flavors, with a crispy shrimp filling enhanced by a honey almond glaze, all tucked into a classic po'boy sandwich.

This Honey Almond Shrimp Po'Boy Sandwich combines the comforting crunch and soft bread of a traditional po'boy with the unique sweet and spicy notes of honey and almonds, offering a satisfying meal that's perfect for lunch or dinner gatherings.

Tips:
- Almond Crunch: Ensure the almonds are finely ground for the coating but save some larger pieces for garnishing to add texture.
- Keeping Shrimp Crispy: Fry the shrimp just before assembling the sandwiches to keep them crispy.
- Sauce Variation: For a spicier kick, add more red pepper flakes to the honey glaze or include a few drops of hot sauce in the mayonnaise mixture

Ingredients:

- *For the Honey Almond Shrimp*:
  - 1 lb large shrimp, peeled and deveined
  - 1/2 cup buttermilk
  - 1 cup all-purpose flour
  - 1/2 cup ground almonds
  - 1 teaspoon paprika
  - 1 teaspoon garlic powder
  - Salt and pepper to taste
  - Oil for frying
  - 1/4 cup honey
  - 2 tablespoons soy sauce
  - 1/2 teaspoon crushed red pepper flakes
  - 1/4 cup sliced almonds, toasted

- *For the Sandwich:*
  - 4 French baguettes or hoagie rolls, split and lightly toasted
  - 1 cup shredded lettuce
  - 1/4 cup mayonnaise
  - 1 tablespoon Dijon mustard
  - Sliced tomatoes
  - Sliced pickles

Instructions:

1. Marinate the Shrimp:
    - In a bowl, soak the shrimp in buttermilk for about 20 minutes to tenderize.

2. Prepare the Coating:
    - In another bowl, mix together the all-purpose flour, ground almonds, paprika, garlic powder, salt, and pepper.

3. Fry the Shrimp:
    - Heat oil in a deep fryer or large skillet to 375°F (190°C).
    - Remove shrimp from buttermilk, allowing excess to drip off.
    - Dredge the shrimp in the almond-flour mixture until well coated.
    - Fry the shrimp in batches until golden brown and crispy, about 2-3 minutes. Drain on paper towels.

Instructions Continued:

4. Make the Honey Almond Glaze:
    - In a small saucepan, combine honey, soy sauce, and red pepper flakes.
    - Heat over medium heat until the mixture is bubbly and slightly thickened.
    - Toss the fried shrimp in the glaze and sprinkle with toasted sliced almonds.

5. Prepare the Sandwich Spread:
    - In a small bowl, mix mayonnaise with Dijon mustard until smooth.

6. Assemble the Sandwich:
    - Spread the mayonnaise-mustard mixture on both sides of the split baguettes.
    - Lay a bed of shredded lettuce on each baguette, followed by slices of tomato and pickles.
    - Top with a generous amount of honey almond glazed shrimp.

7. Serve:
    - Serve the sandwich immediately to maintain the crispiness of the shrimp and the freshness of the vegetables.

Fried Green Tomato and Pork Banh Mi

Difficulty: Medium

Flavor Profile: A fusion of Southern comfort and Vietnamese flair, combining crispy fried green tomatoes with savory pork, and vibrant, tangy Asian-inspired condiments.

This recipe combines classic Southern fried green tomatoes with traditional Vietnamese Banh Mi elements, including savory marinated pork and tangy pickled vegetables, making it a uniquely satisfying sandwich.

Tips:

- Balancing Flavors: The tangy pickled vegetables and spicy mayo complement the richness of the fried tomatoes and savory pork, creating a balanced flavor profile.
- Serving Suggestions: This sandwich pairs well with a light salad or fresh fruit to balance the hearty flavors.

Ingredients:

- *For the Pork*:

  - 1 lb pork tenderloin, thinly sliced

  - 2 tablespoons soy sauce

  - 1 tablespoon fish sauce

  - 1 tablespoon brown sugar

  - 2 cloves garlic, minced

  - 1 teaspoon freshly grated ginger

- *For the Fried Green Tomatoes*:

  - 4 large green tomatoes, sliced 1/4 inch thick

  - 1 cup buttermilk

  - 1 cup all-purpose flour

  - 1 cup cornmeal

  - 1 teaspoon garlic powder

  - 1 teaspoon smoked paprika

  - Salt and black pepper to taste

  - Oil for frying

- *For the Banh Mi*:

  - 4 baguettes or Vietnamese-style French rolls, split lengthwise

  - 1/4 cup mayonnaise

  - 1 tablespoon sriracha sauce (optional)

- *Pickled Vegetables*:

  - 1/2 cup carrot, julienned

  - 1/2 cup daikon radish, julienned

  - 1/4 cup rice vinegar

  - 1 tablespoon sugar

  - 1/2 teaspoon salt

- *Additional Toppings*:

  - Fresh cilantro leaves

  - Thinly sliced jalapeños

  - Soy sauce or Maggi seasoning

Instructions:

1. Marinate the Pork:
   - In a bowl, combine soy sauce, fish sauce, brown sugar, minced garlic, and grated ginger.
   - Add the pork slices and marinate for at least 30 minutes, or preferably overnight for deeper flavor.

2. Prepare the Pickled Vegetables:
   - Mix rice vinegar, sugar, and salt until dissolved.
   - Combine with the julienned carrot and daikon in a bowl. Ensure they are fully submerged and set aside for at least 30 minutes.

3. Marinate and Fry the Green Tomatoes:
   - Soak green tomato slices in buttermilk for 15 minutes.
   - Combine flour, cornmeal, garlic powder, smoked paprika, salt, and black pepper in another bowl.
   - Heat oil in a skillet to 375°F (190°C).
   - Dredge soaked tomatoes in the flour mixture, then fry until golden and crispy, about 2-3 minutes per side. Drain on paper towels.

4. Cook the Pork:
   - Heat a skillet over medium-high heat. Remove pork from the marinade (discard excess marinade).
   - Sear pork slices until caramelized and cooked through, about 2-3 minutes per side.

5. Prepare the Spicy Mayo:
   - Combine mayonnaise and sriracha in a small bowl.

6. Assemble the Sandwiches:
   - Spread spicy mayo inside each baguette.
   - Layer the fried green tomatoes and cooked pork slices on the bottom half.
   - Top with pickled vegetables, fresh cilantro, and sliced jalapeños.
   - Drizzle with a little soy sauce or Maggi seasoning.

7. Serve:
   - Close the sandwiches with the top halves of the baguettes and serve immediately.

Bourbon Teriyaki Meatball Sliders

Difficulty: Medium

Flavor Profile: These sliders combine the sweet and smoky depth of bourbon with the savory umami of teriyaki sauce, enveloped around succulent meatballs, making for an irresistible fusion appetizer.

Bourbon Teriyaki Meatball Sliders are a flavorful twist on traditional sliders, offering a blend of East and West with every bite. Perfect for entertaining, these sliders are sure to be a hit with your guests.

Tips:

- Meatball Size: Ensure that the meatballs are small enough to fit nicely on the mini slider buns.
- Sauce Consistency: If the sauce thickens too much, thin it with a little more bourbon or water until you achieve the desired consistency.
- Serving Suggestion: These sliders are perfect for parties and gatherings as they are easy to eat and can be prepared in advance. Just assemble before serving to keep everything fresh and tasty.

Ingredients:

- *For the Meatballs:*
  - 1 lb ground beef
  - 1/2 lb ground pork
  - 1/4 cup breadcrumbs
  - 1/4 cup milk
  - 1 egg
  - 2 cloves garlic, minced
  - 1 teaspoon ginger, grated
  - Salt and pepper to taste

- *For the Bourbon Teriyaki Sauce:*
  - 1/2 cup soy sauce
  - 1/4 cup bourbon
  - 1/4 cup brown sugar
  - 2 tablespoons honey
  - 1 tablespoon rice vinegar
  - 1 clove garlic, minced
  - 1 teaspoon grated ginger
  - 1 tablespoon cornstarch dissolved in 2 tablespoons water

- *For Assembly:*
  - Mini slider buns
  - Mayonnaise
  - Lettuce leaves
  - Thinly sliced red onion
  - Pickles

Instructions:

1. Prepare the Meatballs:
   - In a bowl, soak the breadcrumbs in milk until absorbed. This helps to keep the meatballs moist.
   - In a large mixing bowl, combine the ground beef, ground pork, soaked breadcrumbs, egg, minced garlic, grated ginger, salt, and pepper. Mix until just combined—do not overmix as this can make the meatballs tough.
   - Form the mixture into small meatballs, each about the size of a golf ball.
   - Arrange the meatballs on a baking sheet and chill in the refrigerator for 30 minutes to firm up.

Instructions Continued:

2. Cook the Meatballs:
    - Preheat the oven to 400°F (200°C).
    - Bake the meatballs for 20-25 minutes, or until they are browned and cooked through.

3. Make the Bourbon Teriyaki Sauce:
    - In a saucepan, combine soy sauce, bourbon, brown sugar, honey, rice vinegar, minced garlic, and grated ginger. Bring to a simmer over medium heat.
    - Add the cornstarch slurry to the saucepan, stirring continuously. Simmer until the sauce thickens, about 2-3 minutes. Remove from heat.

4. Glaze the Meatballs:
    - Toss the cooked meatballs in the warm bourbon teriyaki sauce until they are well coated.

5. Assemble the Sliders:
    - Slice the mini slider buns in half and spread a thin layer of mayonnaise on the bottoms.
    - Place a lettuce leaf on each bottom bun, followed by a glazed meatball, some slices of red onion, and a pickle.
    - Cap with the top halves of the buns.

6. Serve:
    - Arrange the sliders on a platter and serve immediately.

Fried Jalapeño Nuggets and Quick Pickled Daikon Salad

Difficulty: Medium

Flavor Profile: This dish blends the spiciness of crispy fried jalapeño nuggets with the tangy crunch of Asian-style quick pickled daikon. Fresh raw jalapeños and cilantro add an extra layer of brightness and heat, making this salad a vibrant, spicy, and refreshing dish.

This Crispy Fried Jalapeño Nuggets and Quick Pickled Daikon Salad is a delicious fusion of Southern comfort food and Asian-inspired flavors, offering a spicy kick and tangy freshness with each bite. It's perfect as an appetizer or a vibrant side dish for any meal!

Tips:

- Controlling Heat: Removing the seeds from the jalapeños before frying reduces the heat level. For a spicier version, leave the seeds in some or all of the nuggets.

- Pickling in Advance: For deeper flavor, prepare the quick pickled daikon a day in advance and let it marinate in the fridge overnight.

- Crispiness: Serve the fried jalapeño nuggets right after frying to keep them crispy. Avoid mixing them into the salad too far in advance, as they may soften if left in contact with the pickled daikon for too long.

- Flavor Adjustments: You can adjust the sweetness and tanginess of the pickle brine by adding more sugar for sweetness or more vinegar for extra tang.

Ingredients:

- *For the Quick Pickled Daikon*:
  - 1 large daikon radish, peeled and julienned
  - 1 cup rice vinegar
  - 1/2 cup water
  - 1/4 cup sugar
  - 1 tablespoon salt
  - 2 teaspoons sesame seeds

- *For the Crispy Fried Jalapeño Nuggets*:
  - 10-12 fresh jalapeños, seeds removed and cut into 1-inch rounds
  - 1 cup buttermilk
  - 1 cup all-purpose flour
  - 1 cup cornmeal
  - 1 teaspoon garlic powder
  - 1 teaspoon smoked paprika
  - Salt and pepper to taste
  - Oil for frying

- *For Garnish*:
  - Fresh jalapeños, thinly sliced
  - Fresh cilantro, chopped

Instructions:

1. Prepare the Quick Pickled Daikon:
   - In a medium saucepan, combine the rice vinegar, water, sugar, and salt. Heat over medium heat until the sugar and salt have dissolved.
   - Remove from heat and let the mixture cool slightly.
   - Place the julienned daikon in a glass jar or a non-reactive bowl. Pour the warm vinegar mixture over the daikon, ensuring it is completely submerged. Sprinkle with sesame seeds.
   - Let the daikon pickle at room temperature for about 30 minutes, then transfer to the refrigerator to chill while you prepare the jalapeño nuggets.

2. Prepare the Fried Jalapeño Nuggets:
   - Soak the jalapeño rounds in buttermilk for at least 15-20 minutes. This helps to reduce the heat slightly and ensures the coating adheres well.
   - In a separate bowl, mix together the flour, cornmeal, garlic powder, smoked paprika, salt, and pepper.
   - Heat oil in a deep fryer or a large frying pan to 375°F (190°C).
   - Remove the jalapeño nuggets from the buttermilk, allowing the excess to drip off. Dredge each nugget in the flour mixture, coating them completely and shaking off any excess.
   - Fry the jalapeño nuggets in batches, being careful not to overcrowd the pan. Cook until golden brown and crispy, about 2-3 minutes. Remove and drain on paper towels.

3. Assemble the Salad:
   - In a large serving bowl, combine the chilled pickled daikon with the crispy fried jalapeño nuggets. Toss gently to combine.
   - Garnish with fresh jalapeño slices and chopped cilantro for an added layer of heat and brightness.

4. Serve:
   - Serve the salad immediately to maintain the crispiness of the fried jalapeño nuggets.

Thai Peanut Coleslaw

Difficulty: Easy

Flavor Profile: This vibrant salad combines the crunch of traditional coleslaw with the nutty, spicy flavors of Thai cuisine, featuring a creamy peanut dressing that adds depth and richness to this refreshing dish.

Thai Peanut Coleslaw is a delightful twist on the classic coleslaw recipe, offering a combination of textures and flavors that are sure to please any palate, especially those looking for a fusion of traditional Southern and exciting Thai tastes.

Tips:

- Adjusting Flavors: Taste the dressing before adding it to the vegetables and adjust the seasonings as needed. More lime juice can be added for extra tang, or more honey for sweetness.
- Serving Suggestions: This Thai Peanut Coleslaw makes an excellent side dish for grilled meats, such as chicken or pork, or as a vibrant addition to a barbecue or potluck.
- Storing: This coleslaw is best eaten the day it is made as it can become soggy if kept too long. However, you can store it in the refrigerator for up to 24 hours.

Ingredients:

- *For the Coleslaw*:
  - 4 cups shredded cabbage (mix of green and purple for color)
  - 1 cup shredded carrots
  - 1 red bell pepper, thinly sliced
  - 1/2 cup fresh cilantro, chopped
  - 1/4 cup green onions, sliced
  - 1/4 cup chopped peanuts, for garnish

- *For the Thai Peanut Dressing:*
  - 1/3 cup creamy peanut butter
  - 2 tablespoons soy sauce
  - 2 tablespoons rice vinegar
  - 1 tablespoon lime juice
  - 2 tablespoons honey or brown sugar
  - 1 clove garlic, minced
  - 1 teaspoon fresh ginger, grated
  - 1 teaspoon sesame oil
  - 1-2 teaspoons sriracha or another hot sauce (adjust to taste)
  - 2-4 tablespoons water (as needed to thin the dressing)

Instructions:

1. Prepare the Vegetables:
    - In a large mixing bowl, combine the shredded cabbage, carrots, red bell pepper, cilantro, and green onions. Toss well to mix the ingredients.

2. Make the Thai Peanut Dressing:
    - In a smaller bowl or a blender, combine the peanut butter, soy sauce, rice vinegar, lime juice, honey (or brown sugar), minced garlic, grated ginger, sesame oil, and sriracha.
    - Whisk or blend until the mixture is smooth and creamy. If the dressing is too thick, gradually add water until you achieve a pourable consistency.

3. Combine the Dressing with the Coleslaw:
    - Pour the dressing over the coleslaw mixture in the large bowl. Toss thoroughly to ensure all the vegetables are evenly coated with the dressing.

Instructions Continued:

4. Chill and Serve:
    -   Cover the bowl with plastic wrap and refrigerate for at least 30 minutes to allow the flavors to meld and the vegetables to slightly soften.
    -   Before serving, toss the coleslaw again to redistribute the dressing. Garnish with chopped peanuts.

Miso Honey Vinaigrette with Fried Goat Cheese over Southern Greens

Difficulty: Medium

Flavor Profile: This salad features a unique blend of umami from miso and sweetness from honey, topped with crispy fried goat cheese and served over a bed of hearty Southern greens like collards and mustard.

This Miso Honey Vinaigrette with Fried Goat Cheese over Southern Greens salad offers a delightful fusion of Japanese and Southern flavors, making it a sophisticated yet comforting dish suitable for various dining occasions.

Tips:
- Cheese Preparation: Freezing the goat cheese slices for about 30 minutes before breading can make them easier to handle and less likely to break apart when frying.
- Vinaigrette Consistency: If the vinaigrette is too thick, you can thin it with a little water or additional apple cider vinegar for more tang.
- Serving Options: This salad makes a great starter for a dinner party or can be served as a light lunch. The creamy, crunchy texture of the goat cheese pairs beautifully with the robust flavors of the greens and the sweet, umami-packed dressing.

Ingredients:

- For the Miso Honey Vinaigrette:

  - 1/4 cup white miso paste

  - 1/4 cup honey

  - 1/4 cup apple cider vinegar

  - 1/3 cup extra virgin olive oil

  - 1 tablespoon soy sauce

  - 1 clove garlic, minced

  - 1 teaspoon fresh ginger, grated

- For the Fried Goat Cheese:

  - 8 ounces goat cheese, chilled and sliced into rounds

  - 1/2 cup flour

  - 1 egg, beaten

  - 1 cup panko breadcrumbs

  - Oil for frying

  - For the Salad:

  - 4 cups mixed Southern greens (collard greens, mustard greens, kale), washed and torn

  - 1/2 red onion, thinly sliced

  - 1/2 cup pecans, toasted and chopped

- *Optional*:

  - dried cranberries

  - fresh apple slices for added sweetness

Instructions:

1. Prepare the Miso Honey Vinaigrette:

    - In a bowl or jar, combine miso paste, honey, apple cider vinegar, olive oil, soy sauce, minced garlic, and grated ginger.

    - Whisk or shake until well blended and smooth. Set aside to let the flavors meld.

2. Prepare the Fried Goat Cheese:

    - Place flour, beaten egg, and panko breadcrumbs in three separate shallow dishes.

    - Heat oil in a skillet over medium heat.

    - Dip each goat cheese round first in flour, then egg, and finally coat thoroughly with panko breadcrumbs.

    - Fry the coated goat cheese in the hot oil until golden brown and crispy, about 1-2 minutes per side.

    - Remove from oil and drain on paper towels.

Instructions Continued:

3. Assemble the Salad:
    -   In a large salad bowl, combine the mixed Southern greens and red onion slices.
    -   Drizzle with the miso honey vinaigrette and toss to coat evenly.
    -   Add the toasted pecans and, if using, dried cranberries or apple slices, and gently toss again.

4. Serve:
    -   Divide the dressed greens among plates.
    -   Top each serving with fried goat cheese rounds.
    -   Serve immediately to ensure the goat cheese remains crispy.

Coconut Cornbread Crouton Salad

Difficulty: Medium

Flavor Profile: This inventive salad brings a tropical twist to traditional Southern cornbread, using coconut-infused cornbread croutons to add a crunchy texture to a vibrant, fresh salad base.

This Coconut Cornbread Crouton Salad is a delightful fusion that brings together the warmth of Southern baking and the bright, fresh flavors of a tropical salad, perfect for summer gatherings or as a unique side dish for dinners.

Tips:

- Cornbread Texture: For best results, let the cornbread cool completely before cutting into cubes for more even croutons.
- Customization: Feel free to add other tropical fruits like pineapple or papaya to enhance the salad's sweetness and complexity.
- Storage: Store any leftover cornbread croutons in an airtight container at room temperature. They are excellent for snacking or as a topping for other salads or soups.

Ingredients:

- *For the Coconut Cornbread:*
  - 1 cup cornmeal
  - 1 cup all-purpose flour
  - 1/4 cup granulated sugar
  - 1 tablespoon baking powder
  - 1/2 teaspoon salt
  - 1 cup coconut milk
  - 1/4 cup vegetable oil
  - 2 large eggs
  - 1/2 cup shredded unsweetened coconut

- *For the Croutons:*
  - 2 cups coconut cornbread, cut into 1-inch cubes
  - 2 tablespoons coconut oil, melted

- *For the Salad:*
  - 4 cups mixed salad greens (e.g., arugula, spinach, kale)
  - 1 mango, peeled and diced
  - 1 avocado, peeled, pitted, and sliced
  - 1/2 red bell pepper, thinly sliced
  - 1/4 cup thinly sliced red onion
  - 1/4 cup chopped cilantro

- *For the Lime Vinaigrette:*
  - 1/4 cup lime juice
  - 1/3 cup olive oil
  - 1 tablespoon honey
  - 1 teaspoon Dijon mustard
  - Salt and pepper, to taste

Instructions:

1. Bake the Coconut Cornbread:
   - Preheat your oven to 400°F (200°C).
   - In a large bowl, mix together cornmeal, flour, sugar, baking powder, and salt.
   - In another bowl, whisk together coconut milk, vegetable oil, and eggs.
   - Combine the wet ingredients with the dry ingredients, stirring just until blended. Fold in the shredded coconut.
   - Pour the batter into a greased 8-inch square baking pan.
   - Bake for 20-25 minutes or until a toothpick inserted into the center comes out clean.
   - Allow to cool, then cut into 1-inch cubes to make croutons.

2. Make the Coconut Cornbread Croutons:
   - Increase the oven temperature to 425°F (220°C).
   - Toss the cornbread cubes with melted coconut oil and spread on a baking sheet.
   - Bake in the oven for 10-15 minutes, turning occasionally, until golden and crispy.

3. Prepare the Lime Vinaigrette:
   - In a small bowl, whisk together lime juice, olive oil, honey, Dijon mustard, salt, and pepper until emulsified.

4. Assemble the Salad:
   - In a large salad bowl, combine mixed greens, diced mango, sliced avocado, sliced red bell pepper, red onion, and chopped cilantro.
   - Drizzle with lime vinaigrette and toss gently to coat.

5. Serve:
   - Top the dressed salad with coconut cornbread croutons.
   - Serve immediately to ensure the croutons retain their crispness.

Corn and Edamame Succotash

Difficulty: Easy

Flavor Profile: This updated version of the classic Southern succotash features the sweet crunch of corn and the nutty flavor of edamame, making it a vibrant and nutritious side dish that pairs well with a variety of main courses.

This Corn and Edamame Succotash is not only a delightful and easy-to-make side dish but also a healthy option packed with fiber and protein. Its bright colors and fresh flavors make it an appealing addition to any dinner table.

Tips:
- Corn Selection: Fresh corn is preferred for its sweetness and crunch, but frozen corn can also be used as a convenient alternative.
- Flavor Enhancements: For added richness, a splash of cream or a pat of butter can be stirred in just before serving.
- Herb Variations: While basil offers a fresh, aromatic touch, other herbs like cilantro or parsley can also be used based on your flavor preferences.

Ingredients:
- 2 cups fresh corn kernels (about 4 ears of corn)
- 1 cup shelled edamame, fresh or frozen

Ingredients Continued:

- 1 red bell pepper, diced
- 1 small red onion, diced
- 2 cloves garlic, minced
- 1/2 cup cherry tomatoes, halved
- 1/4 cup fresh basil, chopped
- 2 tablespoons olive oil
- 2 tablespoons apple cider vinegar
- Salt and pepper to taste
- Optional: 1 jalapeño, seeded and finely chopped for a spicy kick
- Optional: 1/4 cup crumbled feta or goat cheese for a creamy addition

Instructions:

1. Prepare the Vegetables:
    - If using fresh corn, remove the kernels from the cob. For frozen edamame, ensure they are thawed and well-drained.

2. Cook the Corn and Edamame:
    - Heat a large skillet over medium heat. Add olive oil once the skillet is hot.
    - Add the corn kernels to the skillet and sauté for about 5 minutes until they start to turn golden.
    - Add the edamame to the skillet and continue to cook for an additional 5 minutes, stirring occasionally.

3. Add the Aromatics and Vegetables:
    - Stir in the diced red onion and red bell pepper. Cook for another 5 minutes until the vegetables are soft.
    - Add the minced garlic (and jalapeño if using) to the skillet, cooking for about 1 minute until fragrant.
    - Toss in the cherry tomatoes and cook for another 2-3 minutes until they are just beginning to soften.

4. Season and Finish the Dish:
    - Remove the skillet from the heat. Stir in the chopped basil and drizzle with apple cider vinegar. Mix well to combine all the flavors.
    - Season with salt and pepper to taste. If using, sprinkle with crumbled feta or goat cheese before serving.

Instructions Continued:

5. Serve:
   - Serve warm as a side dish, or allow it to cool and serve it as a refreshing salad. It pairs beautifully with grilled meats or fish, making it a versatile addition to any meal.

MAIN
DISHES

Crispy Rainbow Trout with Curried Carrot Purée and Peanut Salsa

Difficulty: Advanced

Flavor Profile: This recipe offers a complex combination of sweet, savory, and herbal flavors with a Southeast Asian twist. The crispy rainbow trout, curried carrot purée, and vibrant peanut salsa provide a beautiful harmony of textures and tastes, complemented by the creamy richness of coconut lime rice.

This Crispy Rainbow Trout with Curried Carrot Purée and Peanut Salsa is a beautifully complex dish that brings together the rich flavors of Southern comfort food with the bright, zesty elements of Southeast Asian cuisine, making it perfect for a special occasion or elevated dinner.

Tips:
- Trout Skin: Ensure that the trout skin is dry before frying to achieve maximum crispiness. Press the fillets down with a spatula for the first minute to prevent the skin from curling.
- Carrot Purée: You can adjust the consistency of the carrot purée by adding more or less chicken stock. For a smoother texture, pass the purée through a fine sieve after blending.
- Peanut Salsa: Make the peanut salsa ahead of time and store it in the refrigerator for up to two days. This will allow the flavors to meld together for even better results.
- Rice: For an extra layer of flavor, toast the jasmine rice in a little sesame oil before adding the water and coconut milk to the rice cooker.

Ingredients:

- For the Trout:

- 2 rainbow trout fillets
- 1/4 cup salt
- 1/4 cup sugar
- Oil for frying

- For the Roasted Carrots:

- 4 large carrots, peeled and chopped
- 4 shallots, peeled
- 1 whole garlic bulb, top sliced off
- 2 tablespoons olive oil
- Salt and pepper to taste

- For the Peanut Salsa:

- 1/2 cup dried peanuts
- 1 roasted shallot, from the roasted carrots
- 2 cloves roasted garlic, from the roasted carrots
- 1 raw shallot, finely chopped
- 1/4 cup chopped parsley
- 1/4 cup chopped chives
- 1/4 cup chopped Chinese basil
- 1/4 cup chopped Thai mint
- 1/4 cup chopped cilantro
- Juice of 1 lime or lemon
- 2 tablespoons white wine vinegar
- 3 tablespoons olive oil
- Salt and pepper to taste

- For the Carrot Purée:

- Roasted carrots, from above
- 1/2 cup chicken stock
- 2 tablespoons melted butter
- 1 teaspoon curry powder
- Salt and pepper to taste

Ingredients Continued:

- For the Demi-Glace Reduction:
- 2 tablespoons soy sauce
- 1 tablespoon brown sugar
- 1 teaspoon mustard

- For the Coconut Lime Rice:
- 1 cup jasmine rice
- 1 cup water
- 1 can (13.5 oz) coconut milk
- Juice of 1 lime
- 1/4 cup chopped cilantro
- Salt to taste

Instructions:

1. Prepare the Trout:
   - In a small bowl, combine the salt and sugar. Rub the mixture over both sides of the rainbow trout fillets to cure them. Let the trout sit for 30 minutes, allowing the flavors to penetrate the fish.
   - After 30 minutes, rinse the trout under cold water to remove the cure and pat dry with paper towels.
   - Heat oil in a skillet over medium-high heat. Once the oil is hot, fry the trout fillets skin-side down until the skin is golden and crispy, about 3-4 minutes. Flip the fillets and cook for another 2-3 minutes on the flesh side. Set aside on a paper towel to drain excess oil.

2. Roast the Carrots, Shallots, and Garlic:
   - Preheat your oven to 400°F (200°C).
   - On a baking sheet, toss the chopped carrots, whole peeled shallots, and whole garlic bulb (with the top sliced off) in olive oil, salt, and pepper.
   - Roast in the oven for 25-30 minutes, or until the carrots are tender and caramelized and the garlic is soft. Remove from the oven and set aside to cool slightly.

3. Prepare the Peanut Salsa:
   - While the carrots are roasting, toast the peanuts in a dry skillet over medium heat until lightly browned and fragrant, about 3-4 minutes. Set aside to cool.
   - In a blender or food processor, combine the toasted peanuts, one roasted shallot, two roasted garlic cloves, raw chopped shallot, parsley, chives, Chinese basil, Thai mint, cilantro, lime or lemon juice, white wine vinegar, and olive oil. Pulse until the mixture is combined but still slightly chunky. Season with salt and pepper to taste. Set aside.

Instructions Continued:

4. Prepare the Curried Carrot Purée:
   - Transfer the roasted carrots to a food processor along with the chicken stock, melted butter, and curry powder. Blend until smooth and creamy, adding more stock if necessary to reach your desired consistency. Season with salt and pepper to taste.

5. Make the Demi-Glace Reduction:
   - In a small saucepan over medium heat, combine the soy sauce, brown sugar, and mustard. Stir continuously and cook until the sauce thickens and reduces to a glaze, about 5-7 minutes. Brush this demi-glace reduction over the crispy trout fillets just before serving.

6. Cook the Coconut Lime Rice:
   - In a rice cooker or on the stovetop, combine the jasmine rice, water, coconut milk, and lime juice. Cook according to the rice cooker instructions or stovetop method until the rice is tender and fluffy. Stir in chopped cilantro and season with salt to taste.

7. Plate the Dish:
   - To plate, spread a layer of the curried carrot purée on the bottom of each plate.
   - Place a crispy trout fillet on top of the purée, skin-side up to showcase the crispiness.
   - Spoon a generous amount of peanut salsa over the trout for added texture and flavor.
   - Serve with a side of coconut lime rice.

8. Serve:
   - Garnish the dish with additional chopped herbs if desired and serve immediately. Optionally, serve with a simple udon noodle soup, and add a spoonful of peanut salsa to enhance the soup's flavor.

Spicy Catfish with Tamarind Glaze

Difficulty: Medium

Flavor Profile: This dish combines the bold tanginess of tamarind with a sweet and spicy kick, perfectly balanced with crispy fried catfish. The tamarind glaze provides a delightful blend of sweet, savory, and sour notes, while the fish remains tender and moist inside with a crispy crust.

This Spicy Catfish with Tamarind Glaze is a perfect fusion of sweet, tangy, and spicy flavors, combining Southern cooking techniques with vibrant Southeast Asian ingredients. It's a dish that will impress at any dinner table!

Optional Adjustments

- For a milder version, reduce or omit the red pepper flakes in the glaze.
- For extra crispiness, extend the frying time by an additional minute per side, ensuring the fish is fully cooked and extra crispy.

Tips:
- Tamarind Paste: If you can't find tamarind paste, you can substitute with tamarind concentrate or tamarind pulp. Adjust the amount of sweetener (honey) to balance the sourness, as tamarind can vary in intensity.
- Cornstarch Dredge: Using cornstarch creates a light and crispy crust that works perfectly for shallow frying. Ensure that the fish is thoroughly dredged for even crispiness.
- Broiling the Fish: When broiling the glazed catfish, stay close to the oven and watch carefully, as the sugar content in the glaze can burn quickly under high heat.
- Serving Suggestions: You can serve this dish with a simple cucumber salad or a side of stir-fried vegetables to add freshness and crunch to the meal.

Ingredients:

- For the Catfish:
- 4 catfish fillets (about 6 ounces each)
- 1 teaspoon salt
- 1 teaspoon freshly ground black pepper
- 2 teaspoons chili powder
- 1/2 cup cornstarch (for dredging)
- Vegetable oil (for frying)

- For the Tamarind Glaze:
- 1/4 cup tamarind paste
- 3 tablespoons honey
- 2 tablespoons soy sauce
- 2 cloves garlic, minced
- 1 tablespoon fresh ginger, grated
- 1/2 teaspoon red pepper flakes (adjust to taste)
- 1 tablespoon orange juice
- 1/2 tablespoon beef bouillon or 1/2 teaspoon beef bouillon powder

- For Serving:
- Fresh cilantro, chopped
- Lime wedges
- Cooked jasmine rice

Instructions:

1. Prepare the Catfish:
   - Pat the catfish fillets dry with paper towels to remove excess moisture. This step helps ensure a crispy texture when frying.
   - In a small bowl, mix together the salt, freshly ground black pepper, and chili powder.
   - Evenly sprinkle the seasoning mixture over both sides of each fillet.
   - Dredge each seasoned fillet in cornstarch, making sure to coat the entire surface evenly. Shake off any excess cornstarch to prevent clumping.

2. Make the Tamarind Glaze:
   - In a small saucepan, combine the tamarind paste, honey, soy sauce, minced garlic, grated ginger, red pepper flakes, and beef bouillon.
   - Heat the mixture over medium heat, stirring frequently to avoid burning. Bring the mixture to a simmer and allow it to cook for 5-7 minutes, until it thickens into a glaze-like consistency.
   - Remove from heat and stir in the orange juice. This adds brightness and balance to the glaze. Set the glaze aside for later use.

3. Fry the Catfish:
   - Heat vegetable oil in a large skillet over medium-high heat. The oil should be about 1/4 inch deep, just enough to shallow fry the fish.
   - Once the oil is hot, carefully place the dredged catfish fillets into the skillet. Fry the fillets for about 4-5 minutes on each side, or until golden brown and crispy.
   - Use a meat thermometer to ensure the internal temperature of the fish reaches 145°F (63°C).
   - Once cooked, remove the fillets from the skillet and place them on a paper towel-lined plate to drain any excess oil.

4. Glaze the Catfish:
   - Using a pastry brush, generously coat the fried catfish fillets with the prepared tamarind glaze.
   - Preheat your broiler on high. Place the glazed fillets under the broiler for 1-2 minutes, or until the glaze begins to bubble and caramelize. Keep a close eye on the fish to prevent the glaze from burning.

5. Serve:
   - Transfer the broiled catfish fillets to a serving platter.
   - Garnish with freshly chopped cilantro and serve with lime wedges on the side. The lime juice adds a fresh, zesty contrast to the rich flavors of the glaze.
   - Pair the catfish with hot, fluffy jasmine rice, which helps balance the spicy and tangy flavors.

Pecan Crusted Catfish with Yuzu Hollandaise

Difficulty: Advanced

Flavor Profile: This dish features a crispy pecan-crusted catfish paired with a creamy, citrus-infused yuzu hollandaise sauce, blending Southern cooking techniques with Japanese flavors for a refined and elegant entrée.

This Pecan Crusted Catfish with Yuzu Hollandaise brings a sophisticated twist to traditional Southern flavors, enhanced by the exotic, tangy taste of yuzu, making it an impressive option for dinner parties or special occasions.

Tips:

- Handling Hollandaise: Hollandaise sauce can be temperamental. Keep the heat low to prevent the eggs from curdling. If the sauce begins to separate, immediately remove from heat and whisk in a tablespoon of cold water.
- Catfish Preparation: Ensure the trout fillets are dry before starting the breading process to help the coating adhere better.
- Serving Suggestions: This dish pairs well with light sides such as steamed asparagus, a fresh salad, or herbed potatoes.

Ingredients:

- *For the Pecan Crusted Catfish*:
  - 4 catfish fillets, about 6 ounces each, skin on
  - 1 cup finely chopped pecans
  - 1/2 cup panko breadcrumbs
  - 1 teaspoon paprika
  - Salt and pepper to taste
  - 2 eggs, beaten
  - 1/4 cup all-purpose flour
  - Olive oil, for frying

- *For the Yuzu Hollandaise*:
  - 3 egg yolks
  - 1 tablespoon yuzu juice (can substitute with a mix of lemon and lime juice if yuzu is unavailable)
  - 1 stick (1/2 cup) unsalted butter, melted
  - Salt to taste
  - Dash of cayenne pepper

Instructions:

1. Prepare the Catfish:
   - In a shallow dish, combine the finely chopped pecans, panko breadcrumbs, paprika, salt, and pepper.
   - Place the flour in another shallow dish, and the beaten eggs in a third dish.
   - Dredge each catfish fillet first in flour, shaking off any excess, then dip in the beaten eggs, and finally coat thoroughly in the pecan mixture, pressing gently to adhere.

2. Cook the Catfish:
   - Heat a large skillet over medium heat and add enough olive oil to lightly coat the bottom.
   - Once the oil is hot, add the pecan-crusted catfish fillets, skin-side up, and fry for about 3-4 minutes on each side or until the crust is golden and crispy, and the catfish is cooked through. Avoid overcrowding the skillet; cook in batches if necessary.
   - Transfer the cooked catfish to a plate lined with paper towels to drain excess oil.

Instructions Continued:

3. Make the Yuzu Hollandaise:
   - In a heatproof bowl, whisk together the egg yolks and yuzu juice until smooth.
   - Set the bowl over a pot of gently simmering water (double boiler), making sure the bottom of the bowl does not touch the water.
   - Gradually drizzle in the melted butter, whisking constantly until the sauce thickens and doubles in volume. This should take about 3-4 minutes.
   - Remove from heat, and season with salt and a dash of cayenne pepper. If the sauce is too thick, whisk in a few drops of warm water to reach the desired consistency.

4. Serve:
   - Place each catfish fillet on a plate. Drizzle with the yuzu hollandaise sauce, or serve it on the side for dipping.
   - Garnish with additional chopped pecans and a sprinkle of fresh herbs if desired.

Southern-Asian Fusion Salmon with Ghee, String Beans, and Shiitake Mushrooms

Difficulty: Easy

Flavor Profile: This recipe brings together the rich, buttery flavors of Southern cuisine with Asian ingredients, creating a fusion dish that balances sweet, savory, and umami elements. The ghee gives the dish a Southern richness, while the seasoning adds an Asian-inspired twist.

This Southern-Asian Fusion Salmon recipe is a beautiful blend of Southern richness and Asian-inspired freshness, offering a unique flavor profile that combines comfort and sophistication in every bite. The ghee enhances the salmon's tenderness, while the broiled caramelized glaze brings an irresistible finish.

Tips:

- Ghee: The use of ghee provides a rich, buttery base for the dish, adding Southern comfort to the overall flavor profile. You can substitute with clarified butter if needed, but ghee's nutty flavor is ideal for this dish.
- Salmon Broiling: When broiling the salmon, keep a close eye on it as the brown sugar can burn quickly. A quick broil adds texture without overpowering the delicate fish.
- Asian Fusion: The sesame oil, soy sauce, and ginger add a subtle Asian twist, balancing out the sweetness of the brown sugar and creating a harmonious fusion of flavors.

Ingredients:

- For the Salmon:

- 4 salmon fillets
- 2 tablespoons seasoned salt (use a blend of salt, garlic powder, onion powder, and a pinch of cayenne for extra heat)
- 3 tablespoons brown sugar
- 1 tablespoon soy sauce
- 1 tablespoon sesame oil
- 1 tablespoon fresh ginger, minced
- 2 cloves garlic, minced

- For the Vegetables:

- 2 cups string beans, trimmed
- 1 cup shiitake mushrooms, sliced (or use a combination of mushrooms)
- 3 tablespoons ghee (clarified butter)
- 1 teaspoon sesame oil
- Salt and pepper to taste
- 1 tablespoon soy sauce (optional for added flavor)

- For Garnish:

- Fresh cilantro, chopped
- Lime wedges
- Toasted sesame seeds

Instructions:

1. Marinate the Salmon:

- In a small bowl, mix together seasoned salt, brown sugar, soy sauce, sesame oil, minced ginger, and garlic.
- Rub the salmon fillets generously with this marinade mixture. Allow the fillets to sit at room temperature for 20 minutes to absorb the flavors.

Instructions Continued:

2. Prepare the Vegetables:
    - Preheat the oven to 400°F (200°C).
    - In a Pyrex or oven-safe baking dish, melt the ghee by placing it in the oven for a few minutes or by microwaving it until fully melted.
    - In a bowl, toss the string beans and shiitake mushrooms with the melted ghee and 1 teaspoon of sesame oil. Season with salt, pepper, and soy sauce (optional). Mix well until the vegetables are evenly coated.

3. Assemble the Dish:
    - Spread the seasoned string beans and shiitake mushrooms evenly across the bottom of the Pyrex dish.
    - Place the marinated salmon fillets on top of the bed of vegetables, skin-side down. Drizzle any remaining marinade over the salmon and vegetables for added flavor.

4. Bake the Salmon and Vegetables:
    - Place the dish on the lower rack of the preheated oven and bake at 400°F for 20-25 minutes, or until the salmon is cooked through and flakes easily with a fork. The internal temperature of the salmon should reach 145°F (63°C).
    - Once done, remove the dish from the oven and let it sit for 10-15 minutes to allow the flavors to meld.

5. Broil for a Crispy Top:
    - Preheat the broiler on high.
    - Place the dish under the broiler for 1-2 minutes, watching closely to prevent the brown sugar glaze from burning. The broiling will caramelize the top of the salmon, creating a beautiful, crispy finish.
    - Once the sugar is lightly caramelized, remove from the broiler.

6. Serve:
    - Garnish the salmon and vegetables with fresh cilantro, lime wedges, and a sprinkle of toasted sesame seeds for added texture and flavor.
    - Serve hot with a side of jasmine rice or coconut rice to complement the dish's sweet and savory profile.

Crispy Cod with Thai Basil Pesto and Fried Grits

Difficulty: Medium

Flavor Profile: This dish features a harmonious blend of crispy, lightly battered cod paired with a fragrant Thai basil pesto and rich, crispy fried grits, offering a unique fusion of Southern and Thai flavors.

This Crispy Cod with Thai Basil Pesto and Fried Grits recipe offers a delightful mix of textures and flavors, making it a standout dish perfect for a fusion-themed dinner or a special occasion meal.

Tips:
- Grits Texture: Ensure the grits are spread evenly and allowed to set properly to make cutting and frying easier.
- Cod Fillet Thickness: Adjust cooking time based on the thickness of the cod fillets to ensure they are cooked through without burning the crust.
- Pesto Variations: If Thai basil is hard to find, regular basil can be used with a touch of mint to mimic the flavor profile.

Ingredients:

- *For the Cod*:
  - 4 cod fillets, about 6 ounces each
  - 1 cup all-purpose flour
  - 1 teaspoon paprika
  - Salt and black pepper to taste
  - 2 eggs, beaten
  - 1 cup panko breadcrumbs
  - Oil for frying

- *For the Thai Basil Pesto:*
  - 1 cup Thai basil leaves
  - 1/4 cup cilantro leaves
  - 2 cloves garlic
  - 1/4 cup roasted peanuts
  - 2 tablespoons grated Parmesan cheese
  - 1/3 cup olive oil
  - Juice of 1 lime
  - Salt to taste

- *For the Fried Grits:*
  - 1 cup quick-cooking grits
  - 4 cups water
  - 1 teaspoon salt
  - 1/2 cup grated sharp cheddar cheese
  - Oil for frying

Instructions:

1. Prepare the Fried Grits:
   - In a medium saucepan, bring water to a boil. Add salt and slowly whisk in the grits to prevent clumping. Reduce heat and simmer, stirring frequently, until the grits are thick and creamy, about 5-7 minutes.
   - Stir in the cheddar cheese until melted and combined. Pour the grits into a greased baking dish and spread into an even layer. Refrigerate until set, about 1 hour.
   - Once set, cut the grits into squares or rectangles. Heat oil in a skillet and fry the grits pieces until golden and crispy on all sides. Set aside on paper towels to drain.

Instructions Continued:

2. Make the Thai Basil Pesto:
    - In a food processor, combine Thai basil, cilantro, garlic, roasted peanuts, Parmesan cheese, olive oil, and lime juice. Process until smooth. Season with salt to taste. Set aside.

3. Prepare and Cook the Cod:
    - Season the flour with paprika, salt, and pepper. Dredge each cod fillet in the seasoned flour, dip into beaten eggs, and then coat with panko breadcrumbs.
    - Heat oil in a large skillet over medium-high heat. Fry the cod fillets until golden brown and cooked through, about 3-4 minutes per side, depending on thickness. Transfer to a paper towel-lined plate to drain.

4. Assemble and Serve:
    - Place a few fried grits pieces on each plate. Top with a crispy cod fillet.
    - Spoon some Thai basil pesto over the cod or serve it on the side for dipping.
    - Garnish with additional Thai basil or lime wedges if desired.

Blackened Tilapia with Miso Butter

Difficulty: Easy

Flavor Profile: This recipe features the bold, spicy flavors of blackened seasoning complemented by the rich, umami taste of miso butter, creating a delicious fusion of Southern and Asian cuisines.

This Blackened Tilapia with Miso Butter recipe offers a savory, spicy dish that combines the best elements of both Southern and Asian cooking, providing a rich and flavorful dining experience.

Tips:

- Butter Preparation: For easier mixing, ensure the butter is at room temperature before combining it with the miso and other ingredients.
- Adjusting Spiciness: You can modify the amount of cayenne pepper in the blackening seasoning to increase or decrease the heat level according to your taste.
- Storing Miso Butter: Any leftover miso butter can be stored in the refrigerator for up to a week and can be used to enhance other dishes, such as grilled vegetables or other types of fish.

Ingredients:

- *For the Tilapia*:
  - 4 tilapia fillets (about 6 ounces each)
  - 2 tablespoons olive oil
  - 2 tablespoons blackening seasoning
    - paprika
    - cayenne pepper
    - garlic powder
    - onion powder
    - salt
    - black pepper

- *For the Miso Butter*:
  - 1/4 cup unsalted butter, softened
  - 2 tablespoons white miso paste
  - 1 teaspoon freshly grated ginger
  - 1 clove garlic, minced
  - 1 tablespoon lime juice
  - 1 teaspoon honey

- *Garnish*:
  - Chopped fresh cilantro
  - Lime wedges

Instructions:

1. Prepare the Miso Butter:
   - In a small bowl, combine the softened butter, white miso paste, grated ginger, minced garlic, lime juice, and honey.
   - Mix thoroughly until all ingredients are well blended and the mixture is smooth.
   - Set aside at room temperature to allow the flavors to meld together.

2. Season the Tilapia:
   - Pat the tilapia fillets dry with paper towels to ensure proper searing.
   - Rub each fillet with olive oil and then generously coat each side with the blackening seasoning.
   - Make sure the fillets are fully covered with the seasoning for the best flavor.

Instructions Continued:

3. Cook the Tilapia:
    - Heat a large skillet over medium-high heat.
    - Once hot, add the tilapia fillets to the skillet without overcrowding.
    - Cook for 3-4 minutes on each side or until the outside is crispy and the fish flakes easily with a fork.
    - Remove the fillets from the skillet and set them aside on a warm plate.

4. Serve:
    - Place the cooked tilapia fillets on serving plates.
    - Add a generous dollop of miso butter on top of each fillet while they are still hot so that the butter melts beautifully over the fish.
    - Garnish with chopped cilantro and lime wedges on the side.

5. Presentation Tips:
    - Serve the blackened tilapia over a bed of steamed jasmine rice or alongside sautéed vegetables for a complete meal.
    - Drizzle any remaining miso butter over the rice or vegetables for added flavor.

Thai Shrimp and Grits with Lemongrass Butter Sauce

Difficulty: Medium

Flavor Profile: This dish combines the creamy, comforting texture of Southern-style grits with the bright, aromatic flavors of Thai cuisine, featuring succulent shrimp and a flavorful lemongrass butter sauce.

This Thai Shrimp and Grits with Lemongrass Butter Sauce recipe is a delightful fusion of Southern and Thai flavors, offering an exotic twist on a classic dish, perfect for a comforting dinner or a special occasion meal.

Tips:
- Grits Consistency: For creamier grits, feel free to add more water or cream during cooking if they seem too thick.
- Adjusting Spiciness: Control the heat level of the dish by adjusting the amount of Thai red curry paste and red chili according to your preference.
- Serving Suggestion: This dish pairs beautifully with a crisp, dry white wine that can complement the rich flavors without overpowering them.

Ingredients:

- *For the Grits*:
  - 1 cup stone-ground grits
  - 4 cups water or a mix of half water and half coconut milk for creaminess
  - Salt to taste
  - 1/4 cup heavy cream (optional for extra creaminess)

- *For the Shrimp:*
  - 1 lb large shrimp, peeled and deveined
  - 2 tablespoons olive oil
  - 1 teaspoon garlic, minced
  - 1 teaspoon ginger, minced
  - 1 tablespoon Thai red curry paste
  - Salt and pepper to taste

- *For the Lemongrass Butter Sauce*:
  - 1 stalk lemongrass, tough outer layers removed, finely minced
  - 1/2 cup unsalted butter
  - 2 tablespoons lime juice
  - 1 tablespoon fish sauce
  - 1 teaspoon sugar
  - 1 small red chili, finely chopped or a pinch of red pepper flakes
  - 2 tablespoons fresh cilantro, chopped

- *Garnish*:
  - Additional chopped cilantro
  - Sliced green onions
  - Lime wedges

Instructions:

1. Cook the Grits:
   - In a medium saucepan, bring the water (and coconut milk, if using) to a boil. Add a generous pinch of salt.
   - Gradually whisk in the grits to avoid any lumps.
   - Reduce the heat to low and cover, stirring occasionally, until the grits are thick and creamy, about 20-30 minutes.
   - Stir in the heavy cream at the end of cooking for extra richness. Adjust seasoning with salt.

Ingredients Continued:

2. Prepare the Shrimp:
   - In a large skillet, heat the olive oil over medium-high heat.
   - Add the garlic and ginger, sautéing until fragrant, about 1 minute.
   - Stir in the Thai red curry paste, cooking for an additional minute.
   - Add the shrimp and season with salt and pepper. Cook until the shrimp are pink and opaque, about 3-4 minutes per side. Remove from heat and set aside.

3. Make the Lemongrass Butter Sauce:
   - In a small saucepan, melt the butter over medium heat.
   - Add the minced lemongrass and cook until it is softened, about 2-3 minutes.
   - Stir in the lime juice, fish sauce, sugar, and chopped red chili. Bring to a simmer and cook for another minute to blend the flavors.
   - Remove from heat and stir in the chopped cilantro.

4. Assemble and Serve:
   - Spoon the creamy grits onto plates or shallow bowls.
   - Top with the curry-spiced shrimp.
   - Drizzle generously with the lemongrass butter sauce.
   - Garnish with additional cilantro, sliced green onions, and serve with lime wedges on the side.

Udon Noodles with Cajun Crawfish Sauce

Difficulty: Advanced

Flavor Profile: This dish combines the hearty, chewy texture of udon noodles with the spicy, robust flavors of a Cajun-inspired crawfish sauce, making it a unique fusion that is both comforting and boldly flavorful.

This Udon Noodles with Cajun Crawfish Sauce recipe offers a hearty and flavorful experience, perfect for those who enjoy a spicy kick and a fusion of culinary traditions.

Tips:

- Peeling Crawfish: To peel crawfish, twist and pull the tail from the rest of the body. Peel the shell segments from the tail, pinch the tail tip, and gently pull out the meat. Ensure to remove the intestinal tract (a dark vein along the back). Fresh crawfish can vary in size and thickness; adjust cooking times accordingly. If fresh crawfish is not available, you can substitute with pre-cooked frozen crawfish tails. Thaw and add them towards the end of the sauce cooking process just to heat through.
- Noodle Choice: While udon noodles are used here for their unique texture, other types of noodles such as linguine or soba can be used based on availability and preference.
- Sauce Consistency: If the sauce thickens too much or if you prefer more liquid, add more broth to achieve your desired consistency.

Ingredients:

- For the Cajun Crawfish Sauce:

  - 1 lb fresh crawfish, whole

  - 2 tablespoons olive oil

  - 1 medium onion, finely chopped

  - 1 green bell pepper, diced

  - 2 celery stalks, diced

  - 3 cloves garlic, minced

  - 1 can (14.5 oz) diced tomatoes

  - 2 tablespoons tomato paste

  - 1 cup chicken or seafood broth

  - 1 tablespoon Cajun seasoning

  - 1 teaspoon smoked paprika

  - 1/2 teaspoon cayenne pepper, adjust to taste

  - Salt and pepper to taste

  - 1/2 cup heavy cream (optional)

  - 2 tablespoons parsley, chopped

  - 2 tablespoons green onions, sliced

- For the Udon:

  - 400 grams (about 14 oz) udon noodles

Instructions:

1. Prepare and Cook the Crawfish:
    - Bring a large pot of water to a boil. Add the whole crawfish and cook for about 5-7 minutes or until they turn bright red.
    - Drain the crawfish and let them cool slightly until they can be handled. Peel the shells off the tails, remove the meat, and set aside. Discard the shells.

2. Prepare the Udon Noodles:
    - Cook the udon noodles according to package instructions until just tender. Drain and set aside, keeping them warm.

Instructions Continued:

3. Make the Cajun Crawfish Sauce:
    - In a large skillet or saucepan, heat the olive oil over medium heat. Add the onion, bell pepper, and celery, and sauté until the vegetables are softened, about 5-7 minutes.
    - Add the minced garlic and cook for an additional minute until fragrant.
    - Stir in the diced tomatoes with their juice, tomato paste, chicken or seafood broth, Cajun seasoning, smoked paprika, and cayenne pepper. Bring the mixture to a simmer and let it cook for about 10 minutes, allowing the flavors to meld.

4. Add the Cooked Crawfish:
    - Add the peeled crawfish tail meat to the sauce, and stir to combine. Simmer for another 5 minutes, just long enough to heat the crawfish through without overcooking.

5. Finalize the Sauce:
    - If desired, stir in the heavy cream to add richness to the sauce, and simmer for an additional 2-3 minutes.
    - Season the sauce with salt and pepper to taste. Adjust the spiciness by adding more cayenne pepper if needed.

6. Combine and Serve:
    - Toss the warm udon noodles with the crawfish sauce, ensuring that the noodles are thoroughly coated.
    - Garnish with chopped parsley and sliced green onions.
    - Serve the dish hot, with extra Cajun seasoning on the side for those who prefer an extra kick.

Fried Softshell Crab with Mango Lime Aioli

Difficulty: Medium

Flavor Profile: This dish features crispy fried softshell crabs paired with a vibrant, fruity mango lime aioli, combining the classic Southern technique of frying seafood with tropical, refreshing flavors.

Fried Softshell Crab with Mango Lime Aioli offers a delightful mix of crunchy, savory seafood with sweet and tangy tropical flavors, making it a standout dish that's perfect for summer dining or special occasions.

Tips:

- Crab Cleaning: Ensure that the softshell crabs are properly cleaned before cooking. This typically involves removing the gills, face, and apron.
- Oil Temperature: It's important to maintain the right temperature for frying to ensure that the crabs are crispy and not greasy. A kitchen thermometer can help monitor the oil's temperature.
- Serving Suggestions: This dish pairs well with light salads or simple steamed vegetables to balance the richness of the fried crab.

Ingredients:

- *For the Fried Softshell Crab*:
  - 4 softshell crabs, cleaned and patted dry
  - 1 cup all-purpose flour
  - 1 teaspoon paprika
  - 1 teaspoon garlic powder
  - Salt and black pepper to taste
  - 2 eggs, beaten
  - 1 cup panko breadcrumbs
  - Oil for deep frying

- *For the Mango Lime Aioli*:
  - 1 ripe mango, peeled and cubed
  - 1/2 cup mayonnaise
  - Juice and zest of 1 lime
  - 1 clove garlic, minced
  - Salt and pepper to taste
  - A pinch of cayenne pepper (optional)

Instructions:

1. Prepare the Mango Lime Aioli:
    - In a blender or food processor, combine the cubed mango, mayonnaise, lime juice, lime zest, minced garlic, salt, pepper, and cayenne pepper if using. Blend until smooth and creamy.
    - Taste and adjust seasoning if necessary. Refrigerate until ready to serve.

2. Prepare the Softshell Crabs:
    - In a shallow dish, combine flour, paprika, garlic powder, salt, and black pepper.
    - Place the beaten eggs in another shallow dish, and the panko breadcrumbs in a third dish.
    - Dredge each crab first in the seasoned flour, shaking off excess, then dip in the beaten eggs, and finally coat thoroughly in the panko breadcrumbs, pressing gently to adhere.

3. Fry the Softshell Crabs:
    - Heat oil in a deep fryer or large skillet to 375°F (190°C).
    - Carefully place the breaded crabs in the hot oil, and fry for about 3-4 minutes on each side, or until golden and crispy.
    - Use a slotted spoon to transfer the fried crabs to a plate lined with paper towels to drain excess oil.

Instructions Continued:

4. Serve:

   - Serve the fried softshell crabs hot, accompanied by a side of the mango lime aioli for dipping.

   - Garnish with additional lime zest or a sprinkle of chopped fresh cilantro for an extra pop of flavor.

Asian Cajun Seafood Boil

Difficulty: Medium

Flavor Profile: A vibrant and spicy blend of traditional Cajun and Asian flavors, perfect for a communal seafood feast.

This Asian Cajun Seafood Boil is designed to delight with its robust flavors and festive presentation, making it an ideal choice for gatherings that call for something extraordinary.

Tips:
- Adjusting Spice Levels: Customize the amount of cayenne pepper in the spice mix according to your preference for heat.
- Serving Style: For an engaging dining experience, consider serving the boil on a large communal table covered with newspaper.
- Fresh Ingredients: Always use fresh spices for the best flavor impact in your spice mix.

Ingredients:

- *Seafood*:

  - 2 lbs large shrimp, shells on

  - 2 lbs crab legs

  - 1 lb clams

  - 1 lb mussels

- *Sausages and Vegetables*:

  - 1 lb andouille sausage, sliced into chunks

  - 4 corn on the cob, halved

  - 2 lbs baby potatoes

- *Asian Cajun Spice Mix:*

  - 1/4 cup paprika

  - 2 tablespoons garlic powder

  - 2 tablespoons onion powder

  - 2 tablespoons ground ginger

  - 1 tablespoon ground lemongrass (or lemongrass paste)

  - 1 tablespoon ground star anise

  - 1 tablespoon cayenne pepper (adjust based on spice preference)

  - 1 tablespoon black pepper

  - 2 tablespoons salt

- *Herbs*:

  - 1 bunch fresh cilantro, roughly chopped

  - 1 bunch fresh basil, leaves torn

- *Additional Ingredients:*

  - 4 cloves garlic, minced

  - 2 lemons, halved

  - 1 large onion, quartered

  - 4 tablespoons soy sauce

  - 1 tablespoon fish sauce

  - 2 teaspoons sesame oil

  - 6 cups water or enough to cover

Instructions:

1. Prepare the Asian Cajun Spice Mix:
   - In a small bowl, combine all the spices listed under the Asian Cajun Spice Mix: paprika, garlic powder, onion powder, ground ginger, ground lemongrass, ground star anise, cayenne pepper, black pepper, and salt. Mix thoroughly until well blended.

2. Prepare the Boil:
   - In a large stockpot, add water along with the prepared Asian Cajun spice mix, minced garlic, onions, lemons, soy sauce, fish sauce, and sesame oil. Bring to a boil over high heat.

3. Cook Potatoes and Corn:
   - Add baby potatoes to the boiling spice mixture and cook for about 10 minutes.
   - Add the corn on the cob and continue to boil for another 5 minutes.

4. Add Seafood and Sausages:
   - Add the andouille sausage, crab legs, clams, and mussels to the pot. Cook until the clams and mussels begin to open, about 5-7 minutes.
   - Add the shrimp last, cooking until pink and opaque, about 3-4 minutes. Be careful not to overcook the shrimp.

5. Check and Finish:
   - Ensure that all shellfish have opened (discard any that haven't).
   - Turn off the heat and let the seafood soak for an additional 3-5 minutes in the broth to enhance flavors.

6. Serve:
   - Drain the seafood mixture or use a slotted spoon to transfer the seafood, sausage, corn, and potatoes to a large serving platter.
   - Garnish with chopped cilantro and torn basil leaves.
   - Serve immediately with additional lemon wedges on the side.

Smoky Tofu and Turnip Greens Stir-Fry

Difficulty: Medium

Flavor Profile: A hearty and healthy stir-fry featuring smoky tofu and peppery turnip greens, with a hint of Asian flavors.

This Smoky Tofu and Turnip Greens Stir-Fry combines the deep, smoky flavors of seasoned tofu with the fresh, peppery taste of turnip greens, creating a satisfying dish that's both flavorful and nourishing.

Tips:
- Pressing Tofu: Ensure the tofu is well-pressed to remove excess moisture; this helps it absorb the marinade better and become crispy when fried.
- Adjusting Heat: Modify the amount of red chili flakes according to your spice preference.
- Serving Suggestion: This dish pairs well with a light soup or a simple salad for a balanced meal.

Ingredients:

- *For the Tofu*:
  - 1 block (14 oz) extra-firm tofu, pressed and cut into cubes
  - 2 tablespoons soy sauce
  - 1 tablespoon liquid smoke
  - 1 tablespoon maple syrup
  - 1 teaspoon garlic powder
  - 2 tablespoons vegetable oil for frying

- *For the Stir-Fry*:
  - 1 bunch turnip greens, washed and roughly chopped
  - 1 medium onion, sliced
  - 2 cloves garlic, minced
  - 1 red bell pepper, sliced
  - 2 tablespoons oyster sauce (or a vegan alternative)
  - 1 tablespoon sesame oil
  - Salt and pepper to taste
  - 1 teaspoon red chili flakes (optional for heat)

- *Garnishes*:
  - Sesame seeds
  - Sliced green onions

Instructions:

1. Marinate the Tofu:
   - In a bowl, whisk together soy sauce, liquid smoke, maple syrup, and garlic powder.
   - Add tofu cubes to the marinade, gently tossing to coat evenly. Let marinate for at least 30 minutes, or longer if time permits, to absorb the flavors.

2. Prepare the Tofu:
   - Heat vegetable oil in a large skillet or wok over medium-high heat.
   - Add the marinated tofu cubes to the skillet. Fry until all sides are golden brown and crispy, about 5-7 minutes. Remove the tofu from the skillet and set aside on a plate.

Instructions Continued:

3. Cook the Vegetables:
   - In the same skillet, add a bit more oil if needed, and sauté the onion and garlic until they start to soften, about 2 minutes.
   - Add the red bell pepper and continue to sauté for another 2 minutes.
   - Stir in the chopped turnip greens, cooking until they begin to wilt, about 3-5 minutes.

4. Combine and Season:
   - Return the crispy tofu to the skillet with the vegetables.
   - Drizzle with oyster sauce and sesame oil, and sprinkle with salt, pepper, and chili flakes if using. Toss everything together to combine and heat through, ensuring the tofu and vegetables are well coated with the seasoning.

5. Serve:
   - Transfer the stir-fry to a serving dish. Garnish with sesame seeds and sliced green onions.
   - Serve hot, ideally with steamed rice or noodles.

Rosemary and Apple Roasted Chicken (Instant Pot)

Difficulty: Easy

Flavor Profile: This savory and slightly sweet roasted chicken dish is infused with the flavors of rosemary, apples, and a hint of spice from red pepper flakes and Szechuan chili crisps. The combination of sesame oil, ginger, and garlic adds an Asian-inspired twist to this classic roasted chicken recipe.

This Rosemary and Apple Roasted Chicken made in the Instant Pot is an easy yet flavorful dish that combines the warmth of rosemary with the sweetness of apples and the richness of chicken. Perfect for a comforting dinner with minimal effort!

Tips:

- Frozen Chicken: Using frozen chicken is convenient, but ensure the chicken reaches the proper internal temperature. If it needs more cooking time, add 2-3 additional minutes to the pressure cooking time.
- Adjusting Heat: For a milder dish, reduce or omit the red pepper flakes and Szechuan chili crisps. You can also add more chili crisps for an extra kick of heat.

Ingredients:

- 2 tablespoons sesame oil (plus more for drizzling)
- 1 white onion, thinly sliced
- 1 tablespoon minced garlic
- 1 teaspoon bacon salt (or regular salt)
- 4 teaspoons white sugar
- black pepper to taste
- 3 stalks celery, chopped
- 1 tablespoon peeled shredded ginger
- 1/2 teaspoon red pepper flakes (adjust to taste)
- 1 tablespoon Szechuan chili crisps (optional for extra heat)
- 1 tablespoon dried rosemary (plus more for garnish)
- 5 apples, sliced
- 1 lb potatoes, cut into cubes
- 4 frozen chicken breasts
- Fresh rosemary sprigs for garnish (optional)

Instructions:

1. Sauté the Aromatics:
   - Set your Instant Pot to the "Sauté" function and add 2 tablespoons of sesame oil. Once the oil is hot, add the sliced onion and sauté for about 3-4 minutes, until they begin to soften but do not brown.
   - Add the minced garlic, bacon salt (or regular salt), and white sugar. Stir for another minute until fragrant.
   - Add the chopped celery and shredded ginger to the pot. Continue sautéing for an additional 2-3 minutes until the onions become slightly transparent but not browned.

2. Add the Seasoning:
   - Stir in the red pepper flakes, Szechuan chili crisps (if using), 1 tablespoon of dried rosemary, plus salt and pepper to taste. Mix well to combine all the flavors.

3. Add the Apples, Potatoes, and Chicken:
   - Add the sliced apples and cubed potatoes into the pot, spreading them evenly over the sautéed aromatics.
   - Place the frozen chicken breasts on top of the apple and potato mixture.
   - Drizzle the chicken with an additional tablespoon of sesame oil and sprinkle with more dried rosemary for extra flavor.

Instructions Continued:

4. Pressure Cook:
   - Secure the Instant Pot lid and ensure the vent is set to the sealing position.
   - Set the Instant Pot to "Pressure Cook" on high for 15 minutes.
   - After the cooking time is complete, allow the pressure to release naturally for 10 minutes, then manually release any remaining pressure.

5. Serve:
   - Carefully remove the lid and check that the chicken is cooked through (internal temperature should reach 165°F).
   - Plate the chicken with the apples and potatoes, and garnish with fresh rosemary sprigs if desired.

Crispy Fried Udon with Collard Greens and Smoked Turkey

Difficulty: Medium

Flavor Profile: This dish combines the chewy texture of udon noodles crisped to perfection, with the smoky flavor of turkey and the earthy taste of collard greens, all brought together with a savory and slightly spicy sauce.

This dish of Crispy Fried Udon with Collard Greens and Smoked Turkey brings a delightful fusion of flavors and textures, perfect for a comforting meal that's both satisfying and unique.

Tips:

- Noodle Preparation: Ensure the noodles are well-drained and slightly dried before frying to enhance their crispiness.
- Cooking Collard Greens: If the collard greens are too tough, you can pre-cook them slightly in boiling water for a few minutes before adding them to the skillet.
- Adjusting Flavors: Feel free to tweak the amount of chili garlic sauce based on your spice level preference or add more honey for extra sweetness.

Ingredients:

- *For the Udon and Vegetables*:
  - 2 packs of udon noodles (about 400 grams)
  - 2 tablespoons vegetable oil
  - 1 large onion, sliced
  - 2 cloves garlic, minced
  - 1 red bell pepper, julienned
  - 2 cups collard greens, stems removed and leaves chopped
  - 1 cup smoked turkey, cut into bite-size pieces

- *For the Sauce:*
  - 3 tablespoons soy sauce
  - 2 tablespoons oyster sauce
  - 1 tablespoon sesame oil
  - 1 teaspoon chili garlic sauce (adjust based on spice preference)
  - 1 tablespoon honey or brown sugar
  - 1 teaspoon rice vinegar

- *Garnish*:
  - Sesame seeds
  - Sliced green onions

Instructions:

1. Prepare the Udon Noodles:
   - Cook the udon noodles according to package instructions, usually boiling for 4-5 minutes. Drain and rinse under cold water to stop the cooking process. Set aside to dry slightly.

2. Make the Sauce:
   - In a small bowl, combine soy sauce, oyster sauce, sesame oil, chili garlic sauce, honey (or brown sugar), and rice vinegar. Stir well until all ingredients are well integrated. Set aside.

3. Sauté the Vegetables and Turkey:
   - Heat 1 tablespoon of vegetable oil in a large skillet or wok over medium-high heat.
   - Add the sliced onion and minced garlic, sautéing until they start to soften and become fragrant.
   - Add the red bell pepper and chopped collard greens, cooking until the greens wilt and the bell peppers soften.
   - Stir in the smoked turkey and cook until heated through.

Instructions Continued:

4. Crisp the Noodles:
    - In another skillet, heat the remaining tablespoon of vegetable oil over medium-high heat.
    - Add the cooked udon noodles, spreading them out evenly. Let them fry without stirring for about 2 minutes, or until the bottom starts to crisp up. Flip the noodles and crisp the other side, breaking them up as needed.

5. Combine and Finish:
    - Pour the sauce over the crisped noodles, stirring to coat evenly.
    - Add the sautéed vegetables and turkey to the skillet with the noodles. Toss everything together to ensure the sauce evenly coats all ingredients.

6. Serve:
    - Serve the crispy fried udon hot, garnished with sesame seeds and sliced green onions.

Spicy Gochujang Fried Chicken with Bourbon Peach Glaze

Difficulty: Advanced

Flavor Profile: Spicy, sweet, with a smoky bourbon finish. This recipe combines the fiery heat of Gochujang with the sweet and smoky notes of a bourbon peach glaze, creating a complex and delicious flavor combination.

This Spicy Gochujang Fried Chicken with Bourbon Peach Glaze is perfect for those who appreciate a meal with a kick and complex flavors. It's ideal for a weekend treat or a special occasion that calls for something uniquely delicious.

Tips:
- Marinating Time: For the best flavor absorption, marinate the chicken overnight. The acids in the buttermilk help tenderize the meat, allowing the spicy flavors of the Gochujang to penetrate more deeply.
- Frying Tips: Ensure the oil is hot enough before adding the chicken to achieve a crispy exterior without absorbing too much oil. Use a thermometer to check that the oil is around 350°F.
- Safety Note: Be cautious when adding bourbon to the hot saucepan, as it may flame. If you're using a gas stove, consider removing the pan from the flame when adding the bourbon, then return it to heat.
- Serving Suggestions: The spicy and sweet flavors of this dish pair well with a cool, creamy side, such as a cucumber salad or a light coleslaw, to balance the heat and richness of the fried chicken.

Ingredients:

- *For the Chicken*:
  - 4 bone-in chicken thighs
  - 2 tablespoons Gochujang (Korean chili paste)
  - 1 cup buttermilk
  - 1 cup all-purpose flour
  - 1 teaspoon garlic powder
  - 1 teaspoon smoked paprika
  - Salt and pepper to taste
  - Oil for frying

- *For the Bourbon Peach Glaze:*
  - 1/2 cup bourbon
  - 1/2 cup peach preserves
  - 2 tablespoons brown sugar
  - 1 tablespoon soy sauce
  - 1 tablespoon apple cider vinegar

Instructions:

1. Marinate the Chicken:
    - In a large bowl, whisk together the buttermilk and Gochujang until well combined.
    - Season the chicken thighs with salt and pepper. Submerge the chicken in the buttermilk mixture, ensuring it is well-coated. Cover and refrigerate for at least 4 hours, or overnight for optimal flavor.

2. Prepare the Flour Mixture:
    - In a shallow dish, combine the flour, garlic powder, smoked paprika, and a pinch of salt and pepper. Mix well.

3. Fry the Chicken:
    - Fill a deep skillet with oil to about a 1/2-inch depth and heat over medium-high until hot but not smoking.
    - Remove the chicken from the marinade, letting excess drip off. Dredge each piece in the flour mixture, ensuring a complete coat.
    - Fry the chicken in the hot oil, turning once, until golden brown on both sides and cooked through, about 8-10 minutes per side. Internal temperature should reach 165°F. Remove and drain on paper towels.

Instructions Continued:

4. Make the Glaze:
    - While the chicken is frying, combine the bourbon, peach preserves, brown sugar, soy sauce, and apple cider vinegar in a small saucepan.
    - Bring to a boil, then reduce the heat to low and simmer until the mixture thickens into a glossy glaze, about 10 minutes, stirring occasionally.

5. Glaze the Chicken:
    - Once the chicken is cooked and drained, brush each piece generously with the bourbon peach glaze, coating them evenly.

6. Serve:
    - Garnish the glazed chicken with sliced green onions and sesame seeds. Serve hot alongside steamed vegetables or fluffy rice for a complete meal.

Carolina BBQ Thai Lemongrass Chicken

Difficulty: Medium

Flavor Profile: This dish offers a unique blend of smoky, tangy, and slightly sweet flavors with a hint of citrus from lemongrass, finished with a sticky, caramelized glaze.

A fusion of Carolina BBQ and Thai flavors, this recipe combines the best of both culinary worlds, featuring the smokiness and tang of Southern barbecue with the exotic zest of Thai lemongrass.

Tips:

- Lemongrass Preparation: To extract maximum flavor, bruise the lemongrass stalk by smashing it with the back of a knife before chopping. This helps release the aromatic oils.
- Marinating Time: For deeper flavor, marinate the chicken overnight. The longer marination time allows the marinade to tenderize the chicken and infuse more robust flavors.
- Grilling Technique: Keep the grill lid closed as much as possible to maintain a consistent temperature, which helps in cooking the chicken evenly and retaining moisture.
- Safety Note: Always discard any leftover marinade that has been in contact with raw chicken if not boiling it thoroughly for the glaze.

Ingredients:

- 4 bone-in, skin-on chicken thighs
- 1/4 cup apple cider vinegar
- 1/4 cup soy sauce
- 1/4 cup honey
- 2 tablespoons brown sugar
- 1 tablespoon lemongrass, finely chopped
- 2 cloves garlic, minced
- 1 teaspoon smoked paprika
- 1/2 teaspoon cayenne pepper
- 1/4 cup ketchup
- 2 tablespoons fish sauce
- Fresh cilantro, for garnish

Instructions:

1. Marinate the Chicken:
    - In a mixing bowl, combine the apple cider vinegar, soy sauce, honey, brown sugar, finely chopped lemongrass, minced garlic, smoked paprika, and cayenne pepper. Whisk together until well mixed.
    - Place the chicken thighs in the marinade, ensuring they are thoroughly coated. Cover and refrigerate to marinate for 2-4 hours, allowing the flavors to penetrate deeply.

2. Prepare the Grill:
    - Preheat your grill to medium-high heat. Ensure the grill is clean and lightly oiled to prevent sticking.

3. Grill the Chicken:
    - Remove the chicken from the marinade, reserving the marinade for the glaze. Place the chicken skin-side down on the grill.
    - Grill the chicken for about 5-7 minutes on each side, or until the skin is crispy and the chicken reaches an internal temperature of 165°F (74°C).

4. Make the Glaze:
    - While the chicken is grilling, pour the reserved marinade into a small saucepan. Add the ketchup and fish sauce to enrich the flavor.
    - Bring the mixture to a boil, then reduce the heat and simmer until it thickens into a glaze, about 5-7 minutes. Stir frequently to prevent burning.

Instructions Continued:

5. Finish the Chicken:

   - In the last few minutes of grilling, generously brush the chicken with the thickened glaze. Flip and glaze each side to develop a caramelized coating.

6. Serve:

   - Remove the chicken from the grill and let it rest for a few minutes. Garnish with freshly chopped cilantro.
   - Serve the chicken hot with steamed rice, a light salad, or your choice of side.

Yuzu Kosho Roast Chicken with Dirty Rice

Difficulty: Medium

Flavor Profile: This dish features the unique, citrusy heat of yuzu kosho paired with the savory, hearty flavors of Southern-style dirty rice, creating a vibrant and flavorful fusion that elevates the traditional roast chicken.

This Yuzu Kosho Roast Chicken with Dirty Rice recipe combines the zest of Japanese yuzu kosho with the deep flavors of Cajun dirty rice, offering a sophisticated and delicious meal perfect for family gatherings or a festive dinner.

Tips:

- Yuzu Kosho Adjustment: Yuzu kosho can be quite spicy; adjust the amount used according to your taste preference.
- Alternative Cooking Methods: If time allows, marinating the chicken for a few hours or overnight will enhance the flavor infusion.
- Serving Suggestion: This dish pairs well with a light salad or steamed vegetables to balance the rich flavors of the chicken and rice.

Ingredients:

- *For the Yuzu Kosho Roast Chicken:*
  - 1 whole chicken (about 4 to 5 pounds)
  - 2 tablespoons yuzu kosho paste
  - 2 tablespoons olive oil
  - 1 tablespoon soy sauce
  - 1 tablespoon honey
  - 1 garlic clove, minced
  - Salt and pepper to taste

- *For the Dirty Rice:*
  - 1 cup long-grain rice
  - 2 cups chicken broth
  - 1 tablespoon olive oil
  - 1/2 pound ground pork or chicken liver
  - 1 medium onion, finely chopped
  - 1 green bell pepper, finely chopped
  - 2 celery stalks, finely chopped
  - 2 cloves garlic, minced
  - 1 teaspoon smoked paprika
  - 1 teaspoon dried thyme
  - 1/2 teaspoon cayenne pepper (adjust to taste)
  - Salt and pepper to taste
  - 2 green onions, sliced for garnish

Instructions:

1. Prepare the Yuzu Kosho Roast Chicken:
   - Preheat the oven to 375°F (190°C).
   - In a small bowl, mix together yuzu kosho paste, olive oil, soy sauce, honey, and minced garlic to create the marinade.
   - Pat the chicken dry with paper towels. Rub the marinade all over the chicken, both under and over the skin. Season the cavity and outer skin with salt and pepper.
   - Place the chicken in a roasting pan. Roast in the preheated oven for about 1 hour and 15 minutes, or until the juices run clear when the thickest part of the thigh is pierced and a thermometer inserted into the thigh reads 165°F (74°C).
   - Remove from the oven and let rest for 10 minutes before carving.

Instructions Continued:

2. Make the Dirty Rice:
   - While the chicken is roasting, heat olive oil in a large skillet over medium heat. Add ground pork or chicken liver and cook until browned, breaking it into small pieces.
   - Add onion, bell pepper, and celery to the skillet. Cook, stirring occasionally, until the vegetables are softened, about 5-7 minutes.
   - Stir in minced garlic, smoked paprika, thyme, and cayenne pepper. Cook for another minute until fragrant.
   - Add the rice and stir to coat with the vegetable and meat mixture.
   - Pour in the chicken broth and bring to a boil. Reduce heat to low, cover, and simmer for 20 minutes, or until the rice is tender and the liquid is absorbed.
   - Season with salt and pepper to taste. Fluff with a fork before serving.

3. Serve:
   - Carve the roast chicken and arrange on a platter.
   - Serve alongside the warm dirty rice. Garnish the rice with sliced green onions.

Smoked Duck with Hoisin-Molasses Glaze

Difficulty: Advanced

Flavor Profile: Rich, smoky duck with a sweet, tangy glaze that balances the bold flavors of hoisin and molasses.

This dish combines Southern smoking techniques with the deep, complex flavors of hoisin sauce, offering a luxurious treat for special occasions.

Tips:
- Drying the Duck: Ensure the duck is thoroughly dried before applying the rub to help the spices adhere better and to promote crisper skin.
- Monitoring Temperature: Use a reliable meat thermometer to monitor the internal temperature of the duck to avoid overcooking.
- Enhancing Smoke Flavor: For additional smoky flavor, consider adding a pan of water with aromatic herbs and spices inside the smoker. This adds moisture and subtle flavor nuances to the smoke.
- Glaze Application: Apply the glaze in layers to build a deep, rich crust that enhances the texture and flavor complexity of the finished dish.
- Carving the Duck: Allow the duck to rest properly before carving to ensure it retains its moisture. Use a sharp knife and follow the natural contours of the duck for best results.
- Pairing Sides: Complement the rich flavors of the smoked duck with light, refreshing sides like a cucumber salad dressed with vinegar, or a tangy slaw that cuts through the richness of the meat.

Ingredients:
- 1 whole duck, about 5 lbs
- 2 tbsp kosher salt
- 1 tbsp black pepper
- 1 tbsp garlic powder
- 1 tbsp onion powder
- 1/4 cup hoisin sauce
- 1/4 cup molasses
- 2 tbsp soy sauce
- 2 tbsp rice vinegar
- 1 tbsp sesame oil

Instructions:

1. Prepare the Duck:
    - Thoroughly dry the duck with paper towels. Combine salt, pepper, garlic powder, and onion powder in a small bowl. Rub this mixture all over the duck, both inside and out, ensuring even coverage for flavor.

2. Smoke the Duck:
    - Preheat your smoker to 250°F (120°C). Place the duck in the smoker breast side up. Smoke the duck for about 4-5 hours, or until the internal temperature at the thickest part of the thigh reaches 165°F (75°C). If your smoker has hot spots, rotate the duck halfway through cooking to ensure even smoking.

3. Make the Glaze:
    - While the duck is smoking, prepare the glaze. In a saucepan over medium heat, whisk together hoisin sauce, molasses, soy sauce, rice vinegar, and sesame oil. Bring the mixture to a simmer, stirring frequently. Allow it to thicken slightly, about 5 minutes. Remove from heat and set aside.

4. Glaze the Duck:
    - During the last 30 minutes of smoking, start brushing the duck with the hoisin-molasses glaze. Apply a generous layer, and repeat the glazing every 10 minutes until the smoking process is complete. This will build up a rich, caramelized coating on the duck.

Instructions Continued:

5. Rest and Carve:
    - Remove the duck from the smoker and let it rest for at least 10 minutes to allow the juices to redistribute throughout the meat, enhancing its flavor and moisture.
    - Carve the duck, slicing the breast meat and removing the legs and wings.

6. Serve:
    - Arrange the sliced duck on a platter. Drizzle with a little more of the hoisin-molasses glaze and garnish with fresh cilantro. Serve with steamed rice, a simple side salad, or stir-fried vegetables.

Sticky Rice Stuffed Quail with Plum Sauce

Difficulty: Advanced

Flavor Profile: This dish offers an elegant fusion of textures and flavors, featuring tender quail stuffed with aromatic sticky rice and served with a sweet and tangy plum sauce. It's a sophisticated meal that beautifully blends Asian and Western culinary traditions.

This Sticky Rice Stuffed Quail with Plum Sauce is an exquisite dish that's perfect for a special occasion or a gourmet dinner party, offering a delightful array of flavors that are sure to impress any guest.

Tips:
- Handling Sticky Rice: Ensure the rice is well soaked to achieve the right texture and cook evenly when stuffed into the quail.
- Monitoring Quail: Keep an eye on the quail as they cook quickly and can dry out if overcooked.
- Sauce Consistency: Adjust the consistency of the plum sauce with a little water if it becomes too thick.

Ingredients:

- *For the Sticky Rice Stuffing*:

  - 1 cup glutinous sticky rice, soaked in water for at least 4 hours or overnight
  - 1/4 cup chicken broth
  - 2 tablespoons soy sauce
  - 1 tablespoon sesame oil
  - 1/4 cup chopped shiitake mushrooms
  - 1/4 cup finely chopped green onions
  - 1 tablespoon minced ginger
  - 2 cloves garlic, minced
  - 1/4 cup chopped chestnuts or water chestnuts (optional)
  - Salt and pepper to taste

- *For the Quail:*

  - 4 whole quail, cleaned and patted dry
  - Salt and pepper to taste
  - Olive oil for brushing

- *For the Plum Sauce*:

  - 1 cup plum jam or preserves
  - 2 tablespoons hoisin sauce
  - 1 tablespoon rice vinegar
  - 1 teaspoon grated ginger
  - 1 clove garlic, minced
  - 1/2 teaspoon chili flakes (optional)

Instructions:

1. Prepare the Sticky Rice Stuffing:
   - Drain the soaked sticky rice and combine it in a pot with chicken broth, soy sauce, and sesame oil. Cook over medium heat until the rice is tender and all liquid is absorbed, about 15-20 minutes.
   - In a skillet, heat a little oil over medium heat. Sauté the shiitake mushrooms, green onions, ginger, and garlic until aromatic and tender, about 5-7 minutes. Mix in the cooked rice and chestnuts, if using. Season with salt and pepper, and set aside to cool.

Instructions Continued:

2. Stuff and Prepare the Quail:
    - Preheat your oven to 375°F (190°C).
    - Season the inside and outside of each quail with salt and pepper. Stuff each quail with the prepared sticky rice stuffing, but do not overfill.
    - Truss the legs of the quail together with kitchen twine to help hold their shape and keep the stuffing inside during cooking.
    - Brush each quail lightly with olive oil.

3. Cook the Quail:
    - Arrange the stuffed quail in a roasting pan. Roast in the preheated oven for about 25-30 minutes, or until the quail are golden brown and cooked through, and the juices run clear.

4. Make the Plum Sauce:
    - While the quail are roasting, combine the plum jam, hoisin sauce, rice vinegar, grated ginger, minced garlic, and chili flakes in a saucepan. Heat over medium heat, stirring frequently, until the mixture is well combined and slightly reduced, about 10-15 minutes.

5. Serve:
    - Allow the quail to rest for a few minutes after removing from the oven. Cut the twine and gently remove it before serving.
    - Serve the quail on individual plates, drizzled with the warm plum sauce or provide the sauce on the side for dipping.
    - Garnish with additional chopped green onions or herbs if desired.

Coconut-Curry Pork Chops with Asian Pear

Difficulty: Medium

Flavor Profile: These pork chops offer a luxurious blend of tropical coconut and aromatic curry spices, enhanced by the sweet and crisp notes of Asian pear, creating a dish that is both savory and subtly sweet.

This recipe for Coconut-Curry Pork Chops delivers a mouthwatering fusion of flavors, perfect for a special dinner or a flavorful twist on your usual pork chop routine. The creamy, spiced sauce not only enhances the pork but turns this dish into a delightful culinary experience. The addition of Asian pear to the coconut-curry sauce introduces a delightful sweetness that complements the savory spices, enhancing the overall complexity of the dish and offering a unique taste experience.

Tips:
- Adjusting the Sauce: If the sauce thickens too much during cooking, add a little more chicken broth to reach your desired consistency.
- Curry Paste: You can adjust the amount of curry paste depending on your spice preference. More paste will yield a spicier, more flavorful sauce.
- Serving Suggestions: These coconut-curry pork chops pair beautifully with jasmine rice or steamed vegetables to soak up the delicious sauce.
- Meat Temperature: Ensure the pork reaches an internal temperature of 145°F (63°C) for safe consumption and optimal tenderness.

Ingredients:

- *For the Pork Chops*:
  - 4 bone-in pork chops, about 1-inch thick
  - Salt and black pepper to taste
  - 2 tablespoons vegetable oil

- *For the Coconut-Curry Sauce*:
  - 1 can (14 oz) coconut milk
  - 2 tablespoons red curry paste
  - 1 tablespoon fish sauce
  - 1 tablespoon brown sugar
  - 2 cloves garlic, minced
  - 1 inch piece ginger, peeled and grated
  - Juice of 1 lime
  - 1/2 cup chicken broth
  - 1 medium Asian pear, cored and thinly sliced

- *Additional Ingredients*:
  - 1 tablespoon fresh cilantro, chopped for garnish
  - 1 small red chili, thinly sliced for garnish
  - Lime wedges for serving

Instructions:

1. Prepare the Pork Chops:
   - Season the pork chops generously with salt and black pepper.
   - Heat the vegetable oil in a large skillet over medium-high heat.
   - Once hot, add the pork chops and sear until golden brown on both sides, about 4-5 minutes per side. Remove from the skillet and set aside.

Instructions Continued:

2. Make the Coconut-Curry Sauce:
   - In the same skillet, reduce heat to medium.
   - Add the minced garlic and grated ginger, sautéing until fragrant, about 1 minute.
   - Stir in the red curry paste, mixing it with the garlic and ginger until well combined.
   - Slowly pour in the coconut milk, stirring continuously to incorporate the curry paste.
   - Add the fish sauce, brown sugar, and chicken broth. Bring the mixture to a simmer.
   - Add the sliced Asian pear to the sauce, letting it simmer gently and absorb the flavors for about 5 minutes.

3. Cook the Pork Chops in the Sauce:
   - Return the pork chops to the skillet, spooning the sauce and pear slices over them.
   - Cover and let simmer for about 8-10 minutes, or until the pork chops are cooked through and the sauce has thickened slightly.
   - Squeeze the lime juice over the pork chops near the end of cooking.

4. Serve:
   - Transfer the pork chops to plates or a serving platter.
   - Spoon the coconut-curry sauce and Asian pear slices over the chops.
   - Garnish with chopped cilantro and red chili slices.
   - Serve with lime wedges on the side.

Sweet Chili Ribs with Southern Coleslaw in Chinese Pancakes

Difficulty: Advanced

Flavor Profile: This dish combines the savory, spicy sweetness of chili-glazed ribs with a tangy Southern-style coleslaw that's ingeniously incorporated into soft, delicate Chinese pancakes, creating a unique and delectable fusion cuisine experience.

This creative rendition of Sweet Chili Ribs with Southern Coleslaw in Chinese Pancakes encapsulates a delightful blend of textures and flavors, offering a sophisticated and flavorful dining experience.

Tips:
- Consistency of Pancake Dough: Ensure the dough is not too sticky or too dry. Adjust with a little more flour or water if necessary.
- Sealing Pancakes: Make sure the edges of the pancakes are well sealed to prevent the filling from leaking out during cooking.
- Serving Suggestion: These can be served as a main course or a unique appetizer, ideal for showcasing an innovative fusion of flavors at any gathering.

Ingredients:

- *For the Sweet Chili Ribs*:

  - 2 racks of pork ribs (about 4-5 lbs total)

  - Salt and pepper to taste

  - 1 cup sweet chili sauce

  - 1/4 cup soy sauce

  - 2 tablespoons honey

  - 2 cloves garlic, minced

  - 1 tablespoon fresh ginger, grated

- *For the Southern Coleslaw in Chinese Pancakes:*

  - 2 cups all-purpose flour

  - 1 cup boiling water

  - 4 cups shredded cabbage (mix of green and purple)

  - 1 cup shredded carrots

  - 1/2 cup mayonnaise

  - 2 tablespoons apple cider vinegar

  - 1 tablespoon sugar

  - Salt and pepper to taste

  - Sesame oil for brushing

Instructions:

1. Prepare the Sweet Chili Ribs:

    - Preheat your oven to 300°F (150°C).

    - Season the ribs with salt and pepper. Place them in a roasting pan.

    - In a bowl, combine the sweet chili sauce, soy sauce, honey, minced garlic, and grated ginger.
      Brush this mixture generously over the ribs.

    - Cover the pan with aluminum foil and bake for 2.5 to 3 hours, or until the ribs are tender. Baste
      occasionally with the sauce. For a caramelized finish, remove the foil and broil the ribs for the last
      5 minutes.

2. Make the Southern Coleslaw Mixture for Pancakes:

    - In a large bowl, combine shredded cabbage, carrots, mayonnaise, apple cider vinegar, sugar, salt,
      and pepper. Toss to coat evenly.

Instructions Continued:

3. Prepare the Chinese Pancakes:
    - Place flour in a large mixing bowl. Gradually stir in boiling water, mixing continuously until a dough forms.
    - When cool enough to handle, knead the dough on a floured surface until smooth, about 5-7 minutes.
    - Divide the dough into small balls, about the size of a golf ball.
    - Roll each ball into a thin circle. Place a spoonful of the coleslaw mixture in the center of each pancake.
    - Fold over the dough to enclose the filling completely, pressing the edges to seal.
    - Lightly brush each pancake with sesame oil.

4. Cook the Pancakes:
    - Heat a non-stick skillet over medium heat. Place the stuffed pancakes in the skillet and cook for about 2 minutes on each side until golden brown and the filling is heated through.

5. Prepare the Ribs:
    - Once cooked, allow the ribs to cool slightly, then remove the meat from the bones and shred.

6. Assemble and Serve:
    - Serve the shredded rib meat alongside or atop the coleslaw-stuffed pancakes.
    - Provide extra sweet chili sauce for drizzling or dipping.

Sweet Tea Brined Pork Katsu with Miso Mustard Glaze and Apple Slaw

Difficulty: Advanced

Flavor Profile: This dish is a fusion of Southern and Japanese cuisines, featuring tender pork katsu brined in sweet tea for added moisture and flavor, coated with a crispy breadcrumb layer, and complemented by a savory miso mustard glaze and a refreshing apple slaw.

Sweet Tea Brined Pork Katsu with Miso Mustard Glaze and Apple Slaw offers a delightful combination of sweet, savory, and tangy flavors, making it a perfect dish for those who enjoy a gourmet fusion experience

Tips:

- Brining Time: Do not brine the pork for too long as the meat can become too salty. Overnight brining should be sufficient.
- Frying: Ensure the oil is hot enough for frying to prevent the katsu from absorbing too much oil and becoming soggy.
- Serving Suggestion: This dish pairs well with a light, crisp beer or a glass of chilled white wine to complement the flavors.

Ingredients:

- For the Sweet Tea Brine:
- 4 cups water
- 4 black tea bags
- 1/2 cup brown sugar
- 1/3 cup salt
- 1 teaspoon black peppercorns
- 2 bay leaves
- 4 pork cutlets, about 1/2 inch thick

- For the Pork Katsu:
- 1 cup all-purpose flour
- 2 large eggs, beaten
- 2 cups panko breadcrumbs
- Oil for frying

- For the Miso Mustard Glaze:
- 1/4 cup white miso paste
- 2 tablespoons Dijon mustard
- 2 tablespoons honey
- 1 tablespoon rice vinegar

- For the Apple Slaw:
- 2 cups thinly sliced green apples
- 1 cup shredded red cabbage
- 1/2 cup shredded carrots
- 1/4 cup thinly sliced green onions
- 2 tablespoons mayonnaise
- 1 tablespoon lemon juice
- Salt and pepper to taste

Instructions:

1. Prepare the Sweet Tea Brine:
    - In a large pot, bring water to a boil. Remove from heat, add tea bags, and steep for 5 minutes. Remove tea bags and stir in brown sugar and salt until dissolved. Add peppercorns and bay leaves.
    - Cool the brine completely before adding the pork cutlets. Refrigerate and allow to brine for at least 4 hours, or overnight.

2. Make the Pork Katsu:
    - Remove pork cutlets from the brine, pat dry with paper towels.
    - Set up a breading station with three dishes: one for flour, one for beaten eggs, and one for panko breadcrumbs.
    - Dredge each cutlet in flour, dip in beaten eggs, and coat thoroughly with panko breadcrumbs.
    - Heat oil in a large skillet over medium-high heat. Fry each cutlet until golden brown and cooked through, about 3-4 minutes per side. Drain on paper towels.

3. Prepare the Miso Mustard Glaze:
    - In a small bowl, mix together miso paste, Dijon mustard, honey, and rice vinegar until smooth.

4. Prepare the Apple Slaw:
    - In a large bowl, combine sliced apples, red cabbage, carrots, and green onions.
    - In a small bowl, whisk together mayonnaise and lemon juice, season with salt and pepper.
    - Toss the dressing with the apple slaw mixture until well coated.

5. Serve:
    - Slice the fried pork katsu into strips and arrange on plates.
    - Drizzle the miso mustard glaze over the pork katsu.
    - Serve with a side of apple slaw.
    - Garnish with additional green onions or sesame seeds if desired.

Gochujang Glazed Shredded Pork with Asian Pear and Macaroni & Cheese Sushi Roll

Difficulty: Advanced

Flavor Profile: A unique fusion of spicy, sweet, and savory flavors, combining the heat of Gochujang glazed pork with the crisp sweetness of Asian pear and the creamy richness of macaroni cheese in a sushi roll.

This Gochujang Glazed Shredded Pork with Asian Pear and Macaroni Cheese Sushi Roll is a daring culinary creation that beautifully showcases the fusion of Korean flavors with traditional Western elements, all wrapped in a classic Japanese format. It's perfect for adventurous eaters looking for an exciting new sushi experience

Tips:

- Pork Preparation: For the best flavor, allow the pork to marinate in the Gochujang mixture overnight before cooking.
- Rice Consistency: Ensure the sushi rice is sticky and cooled properly to make the sushi easy to roll and cut.
- Serving Suggestion: This sushi roll pairs wonderfully with a light salad or miso soup to balance out the rich and spicy flavors of the roll.

Ingredients:

- *For the Gochujang Glazed Shredded Pork:*

  - 1 lb pork shoulder

  - 2 tablespoons Gochujang (Korean chili paste)

  - 2 tablespoons soy sauce

  - 2 tablespoons honey

  - 1 tablespoon sesame oil

  - 2 cloves garlic, minced

  - 1 inch ginger, grated

- *For the Macaroni Cheese:*

  - 1 cup cooked macaroni

  - 1/2 cup grated cheddar cheese

  - 1/4 cup milk

  - 1 tablespoon butter

  - Salt and pepper to taste

- *Additional Ingredients:*

  - 1 Asian pear, thinly sliced

  - 2 cups sushi rice

  - 2 1/2 cups water

  - 1/4 cup rice vinegar

  - 2 tablespoons sugar

  - 1 teaspoon salt

  - 4 sheets nori (seaweed)

  - Sesame seeds, kimchi, and sliced green onion for garnish (optional)

Instructions:

1. Prepare the Gochujang Glazed Shredded Pork:

    - In a slow cooker, combine pork shoulder, Gochujang, soy sauce, honey, sesame oil, garlic, and ginger. Cook on low for 6-8 hours or until the pork is very tender and easily shreds.

    - Shred the pork using two forks and mix it back into the sauce in the slow cooker. Keep warm until ready to use.

2. Make the Macaroni Cheese:

    - In a saucepan, melt butter over medium heat. Add cooked macaroni and milk, stirring until combined.

    - Gradually add the cheddar cheese, stirring until the cheese is melted and the mixture is smooth. Season with salt and pepper. Set aside to cool.

Instructions Continued:

3. Cook Sushi Rice:
   - Rinse the sushi rice under cold water until the water runs clear.
   - Combine the rinsed rice and water in a rice cooker and cook according to the manufacturer's instructions.
   - Once cooked, transfer the rice to a large bowl. Gently fold in rice vinegar, sugar, and salt. Allow the rice to cool to room temperature.

4. Assemble the Sushi Rolls:
   - Place a sheet of nori on a bamboo sushi mat.
   - Spread a layer of sushi rice evenly over the nori, leaving about an inch of space at the top.
   - Lay out a few slices of Asian pear along the bottom edge of the rice.
   - Add a line of Gochujang glazed shredded pork over the pear.
   - Spoon a line of macaroni cheese next to the pork.
   - Carefully roll the sushi using the mat, pressing firmly to ensure the roll is tight and compact. Seal the edge of the nori with a little water.

5. Cut and Serve:
   - With a sharp, wet knife, slice the sushi roll into 1-inch pieces.
   - Arrange the sushi on a platter and sprinkle with sesame seeds if desired.
   - Serve immediately with additional soy sauce or a small bowl of Gochujang for dipping.

Honey Glazed Sweet Potato Sushi Roll with Quick Pickled Ginger Cucumbers and Sriracha Mayo Red Cabbage Coleslaw

Difficulty: Medium

Flavor Profile: A delightful blend of sweet, tangy, and spicy flavors wrapped in a creamy and crunchy sushi roll.

This sushi roll creatively fuses the comforting sweetness of honey-glazed sweet potatoes with the crunch and zest of quick pickled ginger cucumbers and the spicy kick of Sriracha mayo coleslaw, offering a uniquely satisfying culinary experience.

Tips:

- Sweet Potato Slicing: Ensure sweet potatoes are thinly sliced so they cook quickly and roll easily inside the sushi.
- Rice Cooling: Spread the cooked sushi rice in a large, shallow dish and fan it to cool quickly and give it a glossy finish.
- Assembly: Keep a bowl of water nearby to moisten your hands while spreading the rice on the nori, preventing sticking.

Ingredients:

- *For the Honey Glazed Sweet Potatoes:*
  - 1 large sweet potato, peeled and cut into thin strips
  - 2 tablespoons honey
  - 1 tablespoon olive oil
  - Salt to taste

- *For the Quick Pickled Ginger Cucumbers:*
  - 1 medium cucumber, thinly sliced
  - 1/4 cup rice vinegar
  - 1 tablespoon sugar
  - 1 teaspoon salt
  - 1 tablespoon minced pickled ginger

- *For the Sriracha Mayo Red Cabbage Coleslaw:*
  - 1 cup thinly sliced red cabbage
  - 2 tablespoons mayonnaise
  - 1 tablespoon Sriracha sauce
  - 1 teaspoon lime juice

- *For the Sushi Roll:*
  - 2 cups sushi rice
  - 2 1/2 cups water
  - 1/4 cup rice vinegar
  - 2 tablespoons sugar
  - 1 teaspoon salt
  - 4 sheets nori (seaweed)
  - Sesame seeds (optional)

Instructions:

1. Prepare the Honey Glazed Sweet Potatoes:
   - Preheat your oven to 400°F (200°C).
   - Toss the sweet potato strips with honey, olive oil, and a pinch of salt.
   - Spread on a baking sheet and roast for 20-25 minutes or until tender and slightly caramelized. Set aside to cool.

Instructions Continued:

2. Make the Quick Pickled Ginger Cucumbers:
    - In a small bowl, combine rice vinegar, sugar, and salt, stirring until the sugar and salt dissolve.
    - Add the cucumber slices and minced pickled ginger. Let sit for at least 30 minutes, stirring occasionally.

3. Prepare the Sriracha Mayo Red Cabbage Coleslaw:
    - In a bowl, mix the red cabbage with mayonnaise, Sriracha sauce, and lime juice until well coated. Set aside for flavors to meld.

4. Cook Sushi Rice:
    - Rinse the sushi rice under cold water until the water runs clear.
    - Cook rice with water according to your rice cooker instructions or on the stovetop.
    - Once cooked, gently fold in rice vinegar, sugar, and salt while the rice is still warm. Let the rice cool to room temperature before assembling the sushi.

5. Assemble the Sushi Rolls:
    - Place a sheet of nori on a bamboo sushi mat.
    - Spread a thin layer of sushi rice over the nori, leaving a small margin at the top edge of the nori for sealing the roll. Sprinkle sesame seeds over the rice if desired.
    - Arrange a line of honey glazed sweet potato strips, a few slices of quick pickled ginger, cucumbers and a spoonful of Sriracha mayo red cabbage coleslaw along the bottom edge of the rice.
    - Carefully roll the nori over the filling, using the mat to press and shape the roll. Seal the edge of the nori with a little water.
    - Repeat with the remaining ingredients.

6. Cut and Serve:
    - With a sharp knife, cut the sushi roll into bite-sized pieces. Clean the knife with a damp cloth between cuts to prevent sticking.
    - Serve the sushi rolls with soy sauce, wasabi, and additional pickled ginger if desired.

Fried Chicken, Bacon, and Waffle Sushi Roll

Difficulty: Advanced

Flavor Profile: A decadent blend of crispy fried chicken and smoky bacon wrapped in a sushi roll, then encased in a fluffy waffle batter and deep-fried for a unique twist on classic flavors.

This Fried Chicken and Bacon Waffle Batter Sushi Roll is a daring and indulgent dish that combines favorite breakfast and sushi elements into a single, innovative meal, perfect for impressing guests or enjoying a unique homemade treat.

Tips:
- Ensure Consistency: Make sure the sushi rice is spread evenly and not too thickly on the nori to prevent the rolls from becoming too bulky, which makes them difficult to fry.
- Secure Rolling: Keep the fillings snug within the roll to ensure they stay intact during the frying process.
- Safety in Frying: Use caution when frying to avoid splatters. Use tongs or a frying spider to gently place and remove the sushi rolls from the hot oil.
- Storage: This sauce can be made in advance and stored in the refrigerator for up to a week. Reheat gently before serving.
- Serving Suggestions: In addition to being an excellent dip for the Fried Chicken and Bacon Waffle Batter Sushi Roll, this soy maple syrup sauce can be drizzled over pancakes, waffles, or even used as a glaze for roasted or grilled meats.
- Adjusting Flavors: Feel free to tweak the balance of sweetness and saltiness by adjusting the ratio of maple syrup to soy sauce based on your preference.

Ingredients:

- *For the Sushi Roll:*
  - 2 cups sushi rice
  - 2 1/2 cups water
  - 1/4 cup rice vinegar
  - 2 tablespoons sugar
  - 1 teaspoon salt
  - 4 sheets nori (seaweed)
  - 4 strips of bacon, cooked until crispy
  - 2 boneless fried chicken thighs, seasoned with salt and pepper, and cooked

- *For the Waffle Batter*:
  - 1 cup all-purpose flour
  - 1 teaspoon baking powder
  - 1/2 teaspoon salt
  - 1 tablespoon sugar
  - 1 egg, beaten
  - 1 cup milk
  - 2 tablespoons melted butter
  - Oil for deep frying

-*Soy Maple Syrup Sauce*:
- 1/2 cup pure maple syrup
- 1/4 cup soy sauce
- 1 tablespoon rice vinegar
- 1 teaspoon sesame oil
- 1 clove garlic, minced
- 1/2 teaspoon grated fresh ginger
- Optional: pinch of red pepper flakes for heat

Instructions:
1. Prepare Sushi Rice:
    - Rinse the sushi rice under cold water until the water runs clear to remove excess starch.
    - Cook the rinsed rice with 2 1/2 cups water in a rice cooker or on the stovetop according to package instructions.
    - Once cooked, mix the rice vinegar, sugar, and salt in a small bowl until dissolved. Fold this mixture into the warm rice gently. Allow the rice to cool to room temperature before assembling the sushi rolls.

Instructions Continued:

2. Assemble the Sushi Rolls:
    - Lay a sheet of nori on a bamboo sushi mat. Evenly spread a thin layer of sushi rice over the nori, leaving about an inch uncovered at the top edge.
    - Place a strip of cooked bacon and pieces of fried chicken thigh in a line along the bottom edge of the rice.
    - Carefully roll the sushi tightly from the bottom using the mat, pressing down to compact the fillings within the rice and nori. Ensure the ends are sealed.

3. Prepare Waffle Batter:
    - In a large bowl, sift together the flour, baking powder, salt, and sugar.
    - In another bowl, whisk together the beaten egg, milk, and melted butter.
    - Gradually mix the wet ingredients into the dry ingredients until the batter is smooth.

4. Heat Oil:
    - Fill a deep fryer or large pot with vegetable oil to a depth suitable for deep frying (about 3 inches). Heat the oil to 375°F (190°C).

5. Dip and Fry the Sushi Rolls:
    - Dip each sushi roll into the waffle batter, ensuring it is completely covered.
    - Carefully place the battered sushi roll in the hot oil. Fry until the exterior is golden brown and crispy, about 3-4 minutes.
    - Remove from oil and let drain on a wire rack or paper towels to remove excess oil.

6. Prepare Dipping Sauce
    - While sushi rolls are frying, In a small saucepan, combine the maple syrup, soy sauce, rice vinegar, sesame oil, minced garlic, and grated ginger.
    - If you enjoy a bit of spice, add a pinch of red pepper flakes to the mixture to introduce a gentle heat.
    - Place the saucepan over medium heat and bring the mixture to a gentle simmer. Stir continuously to ensure that the garlic and ginger do not burn.
    - Allow the mixture to simmer for about 5-7 minutes or until slightly thickened. The sauce should coat the back of a spoon lightly but still flow easily when poured.
    - Remove the sauce from the heat and let it cool for a few minutes. As it cools, the sauce will thicken further.

Instructions Continued:

7. Serve:
    - Slice the fried sushi roll into bite-sized pieces while still warm.
    - Serve immediately, serve the sauce warm or at room temperature alongside your fried sushi rolls or other dishes that could use a sweet and savory boost.

Blackened Seared Tuna Sashimi

Difficulty: Easy

Flavor Profile: This dish features the spicy, smoky flavors of blackened seasoning on a seared tuna, served as sashimi-style slices with a clean, fresh finish, blending Southern Cajun techniques with traditional Japanese sashimi.

Blackened Seared Tuna Sashimi is a bold and beautiful appetizer that perfectly marries the heat and herbs of Cajun seasoning with the delicate, fresh quality of traditional sashimi, making it a standout dish for any dinner party or special occasion.

Tips:
- Quality of Tuna: Ensure that you use high-quality, sushi-grade tuna from a reputable source for the best flavor and safety.
- Handling Spices: The blackened seasoning can be intense; adjust the level of cayenne pepper if you prefer less heat.
- Searing Time: The searing time might need to be adjusted based on the thickness of your tuna steaks and personal preference for doneness.
- Serving Suggestions: This dish pairs well with a side of simple cucumber salad or seaweed salad to complement the flavors.

Ingredients:

- *For the Tuna:*
  - 2 fresh tuna steaks (about 6 ounces each), sushi grade
  - 2 tablespoons olive oil

- *For the Blackened Seasoning*:
  - 1 teaspoon paprika
  - 1 teaspoon garlic powder
  - 1 teaspoon onion powder
  - 1 teaspoon ground black pepper
  - 1/2 teaspoon cayenne pepper
  - 1/2 teaspoon dried thyme
  - 1/2 teaspoon dried oregano
  - 1/2 teaspoon salt

- *For the Dipping Sauce:*
  - 1/4 cup soy sauce
  - 1 tablespoon mirin
  - 1 teaspoon wasabi paste, or to taste
  - 1 teaspoon ginger, grated

- *For Garnish:*
  - Sliced green onions
  - Sesame seeds
  - Radish sprouts or microgreens

Instructions:

1. Prepare the Tuna:
    - Pat the tuna steaks dry with paper towels. This is crucial for a good sear.

2. Mix the Blackened Seasoning:
    - In a small bowl, combine paprika, garlic powder, onion powder, black pepper, cayenne pepper, thyme, oregano, and salt. Mix well to create the blackening spice mix.

3. Season the Tuna:
    - Generously coat all sides of the tuna steaks with the blackened seasoning. Press the seasoning into the flesh to adhere well.

Instructions Continued:

4. Sear the Tuna:
   - Heat olive oil in a heavy skillet (cast iron preferred) over high heat until very hot but not smoking.
   - Place the tuna steaks in the skillet and sear for about 30 seconds to 1 minute per side, depending on the thickness. The goal is to sear the outside while keeping the inside raw.
   - Remove from heat immediately to avoid cooking through.

5. Slice the Tuna:
   - Let the tuna steaks rest for a couple of minutes. Using a sharp knife, slice the tuna into thin sashimi-style slices.

6. Prepare the Dipping Sauce:
   - In a small bowl, mix together soy sauce, mirin, wasabi paste, and grated ginger. Adjust the wasabi according to your spice preference.

7. Serve:
   - Arrange the sliced tuna on a serving plate. Garnish with sliced green onions, sesame seeds, and radish sprouts or microgreens.
   - Serve the dipping sauce on the side.

DESSERTS

Ginger Crème Brûlée

Difficulty: Medium

Flavor Profile: A luxuriously smooth custard infused with the warm, spicy notes of fresh ginger, finished with a perfectly caramelized sugar crust.

This Ginger Crème Brûlée recipe elevates a classic dessert with the zesty complexity of ginger, marrying it with the traditional creamy texture and crackly sugar top for a truly sophisticated treat.

Tips:

- Temperature Control: Ensure the cream mixture does not boil when heating. Keeping the infusion gentle will result in a smoother flavor.
- Water Bath: Always use hot water for the water bath to maintain an even oven temperature and ensure gentle cooking.
- Chilling Time: For the best texture, chill the custards in the refrigerator overnight. This allows the flavors to meld beautifully and the custard to set perfectly.
- Caramelizing Top: For a uniformly caramelized top, rotate the ramekin as you torch the sugar to evenly distribute the heat.

Ingredients:

- 2 cups heavy cream
- 1 piece fresh ginger (about 3 inches), peeled and thickly sliced
- 5 egg yolks
- 1/2 cup granulated sugar, plus extra for the caramelized topping
- 1 teaspoon pure vanilla extract
- 1 tablespoon of fresh orange zest

Instructions:

1. Infuse the Cream:
   - In a medium saucepan, combine the heavy cream, orange zest, and sliced ginger. Slowly bring the mixture to a simmer over medium heat, watching carefully to ensure it does not boil.
   - Once simmering, remove the saucepan from heat and let the ginger and orange zest steep in the cream for about 15 minutes to infuse the cream with its spicy flavor.
   - After steeping, strain the cream through a fine-mesh sieve to remove the ginger pieces and the orange zest. Discard the ginger and orange zest and set the cream aside to cool slightly.

2. Prepare the Custard Mixture:
   - In a large mixing bowl, vigorously whisk together the egg yolks and 1/2 cup of sugar until the mixture is light and fluffy. The color should be pale yellow.
   - Stir in the vanilla extract.
   - Gradually pour the warm ginger-infused cream into the egg yolk mixture, whisking continuously to temper the eggs and prevent them from scrambling.

3. Bake the Custard:
   - Preheat your oven to 325°F (163°C).
   - Arrange ramekins in a large baking dish. Carefully pour the custard mixture into the ramekins, filling them nearly to the top.
   - Pour hot water into the baking dish around the ramekins, reaching about halfway up the sides of the ramekins. This water bath will help cook the custard gently and evenly.
   - Carefully place the baking dish in the preheated oven and bake for 40-45 minutes. The custards should be set but still slightly wobbly in the center.
   - Once done, remove the ramekins from the water bath and let them cool to room temperature. Then, refrigerate for at least 4 hours, or overnight, which allows the custards to fully set.

Instructions Continued:

4. Caramelize the Sugar Top:
    - Just before serving, evenly sprinkle a thin layer of granulated sugar over each custard. Use a kitchen torch to melt and caramelize the sugar until it forms a hard, shiny crust. If you don't have a torch, you can place the ramekins under the broiler for a couple of minutes to achieve a similar effect.

5. Serve:
    - Allow the crème brûlée to sit for a few minutes after caramelizing the sugar to let the top harden. Serve with a garnish of crystallized ginger or fresh berries for an additional touch of elegance.

Vietnamese Coffee Pecan Pie

Difficulty: Medium

Flavor Profile: This pie combines the rich, intense flavor of Vietnamese coffee with the sweet, nutty depth of a classic pecan pie, creating a unique and indulgent dessert.

This Vietnamese Coffee Pecan Pie offers a delightful twist on the traditional dessert, incorporating the distinctively strong flavor of Vietnamese coffee which perfectly complements the sweet, caramel-like filling and crunchy pecans, making it a must-try for coffee lovers and dessert aficionados alike.

Tips:
- Vietnamese Coffee Concentrate: To make a strong coffee concentrate, use 2 tablespoons of finely ground Vietnamese coffee brewed with 1/2 cup of boiling water. Allow it to steep until very strong, then strain.
- Pie Crust: For a flakier crust, ensure all ingredients, including the water, are very cold before mixing.
- Preventing Over-Browning: Keep an eye on the pie as it bakes. If the top or edges begin to over-brown, loosely cover with foil to prevent burning.

Ingredients:

- *For the Pie Crust:*
  - 1 1/4 cups all-purpose flour
  - 1/2 teaspoon salt
  - 1/2 cup unsalted butter, chilled and diced
  - 4-5 tablespoons ice water

- *For the Filling*:
  - 1 cup dark corn syrup
  - 1/2 cup granulated sugar
  - 1/2 cup brown sugar
  - 3 large eggs
  - 3 tablespoons unsalted butter, melted
  - 2 teaspoons pure vanilla extract
  - 2 tablespoons Vietnamese coffee concentrate (strong brewed Vietnamese coffee)
  - 1 1/2 cups pecan halves
  - 1 teaspoon salt

Instructions:

1. Prepare the Pie Crust:
   - In a large bowl, combine flour and salt.
   - Cut in chilled butter using a pastry blender or two forks until the mixture resembles coarse crumbs.
   - Gradually add ice water, stirring with a fork, until the dough just begins to clump together.
   - Turn the dough out onto a work surface and press together into a ball. Flatten into a disk, wrap in plastic, and refrigerate for at least 30 minutes.

2. Roll Out the Dough:
   - On a lightly floured surface, roll out the dough to fit a 9-inch pie plate.
   - Transfer the rolled dough to the pie plate, trim the edges, and crimp as desired. Chill in the refrigerator while preparing the filling.

3. Make the Filling:
   - In a large bowl, whisk together corn syrup, granulated sugar, brown sugar, and eggs until smooth.
   - Stir in melted butter, vanilla extract, Vietnamese coffee concentrate, and salt until well combined.
   - Mix in the pecan halves.

Instructions Continued:

4. Assemble and Bake:
    - Preheat your oven to 350°F (175°C).
    - Pour the filling into the chilled pie crust.
    - Place the pie on a baking sheet and bake for 50-60 minutes, or until the filling is set and the crust is golden brown. If the edges of the crust begin to brown too quickly, cover them with foil.
    - Remove the pie from the oven and let it cool on a wire rack for at least 2 hours before serving.

5. Serve:
    - Cut into slices and serve at room temperature or slightly warmed.
    - Optional: Serve with a dollop of whipped cream or a scoop of vanilla ice cream.

Matcha Sea Salt Caramel Corn

Difficulty: Easy

Flavor Profile: This unique snack combines the earthy tones of matcha green tea with the rich sweetness of caramel and a hint of sea salt for a perfect balance of flavor. It's a delightful twist on traditional caramel corn that adds an Asian-inspired complexity.

This Matcha Sea Salt Caramel Corn is an exceptional treat that marries traditional snack elements with the refined taste of matcha, making it a standout choice for gatherings, movie nights, or when you crave a sweet and salty snack with a twist.

Tips:
- Handling Caramel: Be very careful when working with hot caramel, as it is extremely hot and can cause burns if it comes into contact with skin.
- Matcha Quality: Use high-quality matcha powder for the best flavor, as it will provide a vibrant color and superior taste.
- Serving Suggestion: Matcha sea salt caramel corn makes an excellent gift or party snack. Package it in clear bags tied with a ribbon for a charming presentation.

Ingredients:

- *For the Caramel Sauce:*
  - 1 cup granulated sugar
  - 1/4 cup water
  - 1/2 cup heavy cream
  - 1/4 cup unsalted butter
  - 1 teaspoon sea salt
  - 1 tablespoon matcha powder

- *For the Popcorn:*
  - 1/2 cup popcorn kernels
  - 2 tablespoons vegetable oil (for popping)
  - Additional sea salt, for sprinkling

Instructions:

1. Pop the Corn:
   - In a large pot with a lid, heat the vegetable oil over medium-high heat.
   - Add the popcorn kernels and cover the pot. Once the kernels begin to pop, shake the pot occasionally to prevent the kernels from burning.
   - When the popping slows down to several seconds between pops, remove the pot from heat. Uncover and transfer the popcorn to a large bowl, discarding any unpopped kernels.

2. Prepare the Matcha Caramel Sauce:
   - In a small bowl, dissolve the matcha powder in a little bit of heavy cream to create a smooth paste.
   - In a medium saucepan, combine sugar and water over medium heat. Stir gently until the sugar dissolves completely.
   - Increase the heat to high and bring the mixture to a boil without stirring, until the syrup becomes a deep amber color, about 6-8 minutes.
   - Remove the saucepan from the heat and carefully whisk in the remaining heavy cream. The mixture will bubble vigorously.
   - Stir in the butter, sea salt, and matcha paste until smooth.

3. Coat the Popcorn:
   - Pour the warm matcha caramel sauce over the popped popcorn in the bowl. Use a spatula to gently toss the popcorn with the caramel, ensuring each piece is evenly coated.
   - Spread the coated popcorn on a large baking sheet lined with parchment paper or a silicone mat.

Instructions Continued:

4. Bake the Caramel Corn:
    - Preheat your oven to 250°F (120°C).
    - Bake the caramel corn for 45 minutes, stirring every 15 minutes to ensure even coating and to prevent clumps.
    - Remove from the oven and sprinkle lightly with additional sea salt while still warm.

5. Cool and Serve:
    - Allow the caramel corn to cool completely on the baking sheet. It will crisp up as it cools.
    - Break apart any large clumps and serve, or store in an airtight container for up to a week.

Lychee Goji Berry and Shredded Ginger Carrot Cake

Difficulty: Medium

Flavor Profile: A twist on the classic carrot cake, this version incorporates the exotic, floral sweetness of lychee, the tartness of goji berries, and the warmth of freshly shredded ginger. The cake is moist, spiced, and filled with unique flavors that bring an Asian fusion flair to a traditional favorite.

This Lychee and Goji Berry Carrot Cake with Shredded Ginger brings an exciting twist to a traditional favorite, making it perfect for gatherings where you want to impress with both flavor and creativity.

Tips:

- Lychee Fruit: If fresh lychee is unavailable, canned lychee can be used. Make sure to drain them thoroughly before chopping to avoid excess moisture in the batter.
- Goji Berries: Soak the goji berries in warm water for 10-15 minutes to rehydrate them before adding to the batter. This will prevent them from becoming too chewy during baking.
- If Goji Berries are unavailable you can use 1 cup of golden raisins. If Lychees are unavailable you can use an 8 oz can of crushed pineapple with the liquid drained
- Frosting Consistency: If the frosting is too thick, add a bit more cream. If it's too thin, sift in a little more confectioners' sugar until it reaches the desired consistency.
- Cool butter and eggs to room temperature before using in batter or frosting
- Decorating: For a more polished look, use a bench scraper to smooth the frosting on the sides of the cake before decorating with nuts or piped frosting.

Ingredients:

- *For the Cake*:
  - 1 1/2 cups granulated white sugar
  - 1/2 cup packed light brown sugar
  - 1 cup vegetable oil (or high-quality olive oil)
  - 1 stick unsalted butter
  - 3 large eggs
  - 1 tablespoon pure vanilla extract
  - 2 1/2 cups all-purpose flour
  - 2 teaspoons baking powder
  - 1/2 teaspoon baking soda
  - 2 teaspoons ground cinnamon
  - 1/2 teaspoon salt
  - 2 cups shredded carrots
  - 8 oz fresh lychee fruit, peeled and seeds removed, finely chopped
  - 1 cup dried goji berries (soaked in warm water for 10 minutes, then drained)
  - 1 tablespoon freshly shredded ginger
  - 1 cup chopped toasted walnuts

- *For the Cream Cheese Frosting*:
  - 2 packages Philadelphia brand cream cheese, softened
  - 1 stick unsalted butter, room temperature
  - 1 1/2 teaspoons pure vanilla extract
  - 1 1/2 cups confectioners' sugar, sifted
  - 1/4 cup heavy whipping cream

Instructions:

1. Preheat the Oven:
   - Preheat your oven to 350°F (175°C). Grease a 3 qt glass baking dish

2. Brown the Butter:
   - In a saucepan, melt butter on medium heat stirring continuously
   - Continue cooking until browned. Browned butter can burn quickly so remove from heat as soon as it turns golden brown and has a nutty aroma

Instructions Continued:

3. Prepare the Cake Batter:
   - In a large mixing bowl, beat the granulated sugar, brown sugar, oil, brown butter, eggs, and vanilla extract until well blended and smooth.
   - In a separate bowl, whisk together the flour, baking powder, baking soda, cinnamon, and salt.
   - Gradually add the dry ingredients into the wet sugar mixture, stirring until fully combined.

4. Incorporate the Add-Ins:
   - Gently fold in the shredded carrots, chopped lychee, drained goji berries, shredded ginger, and chopped toasted walnuts until evenly distributed throughout the batter.

5. Bake the Cake:
   - Pour the cake batter into a greased 3 qt glass baking dish
   - Bake in the oven preheated to 350° F oven for 40 to 45 minutes, or until a toothpick inserted into the center of the cakes comes out clean.
   - If you have access to a combi oven, cook at 20% humidity. If not you can add a small metal container of water in the oven on a lower shelf when you insert the cake
   - Remove from the oven and allow the cakes to cool in the pan completely. Once cooled to room temperature, cover in plastic wrap and transfer to fridge

6. Make the Cream Cheese Frosting:
   - In the bowl of a stand mixer (or using a hand mixer), beat the softened cream cheese and butter together until creamy and smooth.
   - Add the vanilla extract and gradually mix in the confectioners' sugar, 1/2 cup at a time, until fully incorporated.
   - Slowly add the heavy whipping cream, 1 tablespoon at a time, beating until the frosting becomes smooth, creamy, and spreadable.

7. Assemble the Cake:
   - Cover top of cooled cake with icing. Sprinkle some additional chopped toasted walnuts on top

Black Sesame Banana Bread Pudding

Difficulty: Medium

Flavor Profile: This dessert blends the nutty, earthy notes of black sesame with the sweet, comforting flavors of banana bread pudding, creating a rich and unique twist on a classic Southern dessert.

This Black Sesame Banana Bread Pudding is an indulgent and globally inspired dessert that elegantly fuses Asian flavors with a traditional Southern favorite, perfect for any occasion where you want to impress your guests.

Tips:
- Bread Selection: Using slightly stale banana bread helps in absorbing more of the custard without becoming too soggy.
- Black Sesame Paste: If black sesame paste is not available, you can make a simple version by blending toasted black sesame seeds with a bit of sesame oil until smooth.
- Serving Suggestions: This dessert pairs beautifully with a scoop of vanilla or coconut ice cream, adding a cool contrast to the warm pudding.
- Storing: This bread pudding can be stored in the refrigerator for up to 3 days and reheats well in the microwave, making it a great make-ahead dessert option.

Ingredients:

- *For the Banana Bread Pudding:*
  - 8 cups cubed banana bread (preferably stale or dried out)
  - 3 ripe bananas, mashed
  - 3 cups whole milk
  - 1 cup heavy cream
  - 4 large eggs
  - 3/4 cup granulated sugar
  - 1 tablespoon vanilla extract
  - 2 tablespoons black sesame paste (can be found in Asian grocery stores or made by grinding black sesame seeds)

- *For the Black Sesame Sauce:*
  - 1/4 cup black sesame seeds
  - 1/2 cup sugar
  - 1/2 cup water
  - 1 tablespoon butter

- *For Garnish:*
  - Whole black sesame seeds for sprinkling
  - Sliced bananas, optional

Instructions:

1. Prepare the Bread Pudding:
   - Preheat your oven to 350°F (175°C).
   - In a large mixing bowl, whisk together the milk, heavy cream, eggs, sugar, vanilla extract, and black sesame paste until fully combined.
   - Stir in the mashed bananas.
   - Add the cubed banana bread to the mixture, making sure each piece is well-coated. Let sit for about 15 minutes to allow the bread to absorb the custard.
   - Pour the mixture into a greased 9x13 inch baking dish, spreading evenly.

2. Bake the Bread Pudding:
   - Place the baking dish in the preheated oven and bake for 45-50 minutes, or until the top is golden brown and the center is set (test by inserting a knife; it should come out clean).

Instructions Continued:

3. Make the Black Sesame Sauce:
    - While the bread pudding is baking, toast the black sesame seeds in a dry skillet over medium heat until fragrant, about 3-5 minutes, stirring constantly to avoid burning.
    - Grind the toasted sesame seeds with sugar in a spice grinder or with a mortar and pestle until smooth.
    - In a small saucepan, combine the ground sesame sugar with water. Bring to a simmer over medium heat, stirring until the sugar dissolves.
    - Add the butter and stir until melted and the sauce is smooth.

4. Serve:
    - Once the bread pudding is done, let it cool slightly. Serve warm, drizzled with the black sesame sauce.
    - Garnish with additional black sesame seeds and, if desired, freshly sliced bananas.

Ube and Honey Biscuits with Chai Spiced Cream

Difficulty: Advanced

Flavor Profile: This dessert combines the vibrant, sweet taste of ube (purple yam) with the soothing flavors of honey and chai-spiced cream, creating a unique and enticing fusion of flavors.

Ube and Honey Biscuits with Chai Spiced Cream offer a delightful twist on classic Southern biscuits, incorporating the exotic flavors of ube and chai for a truly memorable dessert experience.

Tips:
- Working with Ube: Ube halaya (jam) can vary in sweetness and consistency. Adjust the amount of honey and buttermilk based on the sweetness and thickness of your ube halaya.
- Handling Biscuit Dough: Handle the dough as little as possible to keep the biscuits tender. Overworking the dough can result in tough biscuits.
- Chai Spice Adjustments: Feel free to adjust the chai spices according to your taste preferences. Some might prefer more cinnamon or a hint more ginger.
- Storing: These biscuits are best enjoyed fresh but can be stored in an airtight container at room temperature for up to 2 days. Reheat in the oven or microwave before serving.

Ingredients:

- *For the Ube and Honey Biscuits:*
  - 2 cups all-purpose flour
  - 1 tablespoon baking powder
  - 1/2 teaspoon salt
  - 1/4 cup sugar
  - 1/2 cup cold butter, cubed
  - 1/2 cup ube halaya (ube jam, available in Asian markets)
  - 1/4 cup honey
  - 3/4 cup buttermilk

- *For the Chai Spiced Cream:*
  - 1 cup heavy cream
  - 1/4 cup powdered sugar
  - 1 teaspoon ground cinnamon
  - 1/2 teaspoon ground cardamom
  - 1/4 teaspoon ground ginger
  - 1/4 teaspoon ground cloves
  - 1/4 teaspoon ground nutmeg

Instructions:

1. Prepare the Ube and Honey Biscuits:
   - Preheat your oven to 425°F (220°C).
   - In a large bowl, whisk together flour, baking powder, salt, and sugar.
   - Add the cold cubed butter to the flour mixture. Using a pastry cutter or your fingertips, work the butter into the flour until the mixture resembles coarse crumbs.
   - In a separate bowl, mix together the ube halaya, honey, and buttermilk until well combined.
   - Gradually add the ube mixture to the dry ingredients, stirring until just combined. The dough will be sticky.
   - Turn the dough out onto a floured surface, and gently knead just until it comes together. Roll the dough to about 1-inch thickness.
   - Using a biscuit cutter or a glass, cut out biscuits and place them on a baking sheet lined with parchment paper.
   - Bake for 12-15 minutes or until the biscuits are risen and golden brown.

Instructions Continued:

2. Make the Chai Spiced Cream:
    - In a mixing bowl, combine heavy cream and powdered sugar.
    - Using an electric mixer, whip the cream until it begins to thicken.
    - Add the cinnamon, cardamom, ginger, cloves, and nutmeg. Continue to whip until the cream forms stiff peaks.

3. Serve:
    - Serve the warm ube and honey biscuits with a generous dollop of chai spiced cream on top or on the side for dipping.
    - Garnish with a light drizzle of honey if desired.

Miso Butterscotch Brownies

Difficulty: Medium

Flavor Profile: These brownies meld the rich, fudgy sweetness of traditional brownies with the salty, umami depth of miso and the caramel-like flavors of butterscotch, creating a complex and irresistible dessert.

Miso Butterscotch Brownies are a delightful fusion dessert that combines traditional sweet treats with a savory twist, perfect for those who enjoy exploring unique flavor combinations in their baking.

Tips:
- Miso Paste: White miso is recommended for its mild flavor, which complements rather than overwhelms the sweet elements of the dessert.
- Butterscotch Consistency: Ensure the butterscotch is not too runny before swirling; a thicker consistency will stay in place and create beautiful swirls.
- Checking Doneness: Be careful not to overbake the brownies; they should be soft and fudgy. Start checking for doneness after 25 minutes.
- Storage: These brownies can be stored in an airtight container at room temperature for up to 3 days or refrigerated for a week.

Ingredients:

- *For the Brownie Batter:*
  - 1 cup all-purpose flour
  - 1/2 teaspoon salt
  - 2 tablespoons dark cocoa powder
  - 2/3 cup unsalted butter
  - 1/2 cup semisweet chocolate chips
  - 1 cup granulated sugar
  - 1/2 cup brown sugar
  - 2 tablespoons white miso paste
  - 3 large eggs
  - 2 teaspoons vanilla extract

- *For the Butterscotch Swirl:*
  - 1/4 cup unsalted butter
  - 1/2 cup packed brown sugar
  - 1/3 cup heavy cream
  - 1 teaspoon vanilla extract
  - 1/2 teaspoon salt

Instructions:

1. Prepare the Brownie Batter:
   - Preheat your oven to 350°F (175°C). Line an 8x8 inch baking pan with parchment paper, leaving an overhang on the sides for easy removal.
   - In a medium bowl, whisk together flour, salt, and cocoa powder. Set aside.
   - In a saucepan over low heat, melt the butter and chocolate chips together, stirring until smooth.
   - Remove from heat and whisk in granulated sugar, brown sugar, and miso paste until well combined.
   - Add the eggs, one at a time, whisking well after each addition. Stir in the vanilla extract.
   - Gradually fold in the dry ingredients until just combined. Avoid overmixing.

2. Make the Butterscotch Swirl:
   - In a small saucepan, melt the butter over medium heat.
   - Add the brown sugar and stir until the sugar has dissolved and the mixture starts to bubble.
   - Slowly pour in the heavy cream while stirring continuously. Bring the mixture to a gentle boil and let it cook for about one minute.
   - Remove from heat and stir in vanilla extract and salt. Set aside to cool slightly.

Instructions Continued:

3. Assemble and Bake:
    - Pour the brownie batter into the prepared baking pan. Drop spoonfuls of the butterscotch mixture on top of the brownie batter.
    - Using a knife or a toothpick, swirl the butterscotch into the brownie batter, creating a marbled effect.
    - Bake in the preheated oven for 25-30 minutes, or until a toothpick inserted into the center comes out with just a few moist crumbs.
    - Remove from the oven and allow to cool completely in the pan set on a wire rack.

4. Serve:
    - Lift the brownies out of the pan using the parchment paper overhang. Cut into squares.
    - Serve as is, or with a scoop of vanilla ice cream for an added treat.

Black Tea Custard with Ginger Snap Crust

Difficulty: Medium

Flavor Profile: This dessert offers a harmonious blend of robust black tea infused custard paired with a spicy, crunchy ginger snap crust. The unique combination of aromatic tea with the zesty snap of ginger creates a sophisticated and memorable dessert.

This Black Tea Custard with Ginger Snap Crust is a delightful dessert that combines the comforting warmth of tea and spices with the rich, creamy texture of custard, perfect for a refined ending to any meal.

Tips:

- Crust Thickness: Ensure the crust is not too thick, especially at the bottom, to allow a nice balance with the custard.
- Tea Steeping: Be careful not to over-steep the tea, as it can become bitter. Taste the cream mixture after 10 minutes to check the flavor strength.
- Custard Consistency: Constant stirring while cooking the custard is crucial to avoid lumps and ensure a smooth texture.
- Serving Suggestion: For an extra touch of elegance, serve with a side of candied ginger or a drizzle of honey.

Ingredients:

- *For the Ginger Snap Crust:*
  - 1 1/2 cups ginger snap cookies, crushed
  - 1/4 cup unsalted butter, melted
  - 1 tablespoon sugar

- *For the Black Tea Custard:*
  - 2 cups heavy cream
  - 1/2 cup whole milk
  - 1/4 cup granulated sugar
  - 3 tablespoons loose black tea leaves or 4 black tea bags
  - 6 egg yolks
  - 1/4 cup granulated sugar (additional for the custard mixture)
  - 1 teaspoon vanilla extract

Instructions:

1. Prepare the Ginger Snap Crust:
   - Preheat your oven to 350°F (175°C).
   - In a mixing bowl, combine crushed ginger snap cookies, melted butter, and sugar until well mixed.
   - Press the mixture evenly into the bottom and slightly up the sides of a 9-inch pie dish or tart pan.
   - Bake in the preheated oven for about 8-10 minutes until set and slightly darker in color. Remove from the oven and allow to cool completely.

2. Make the Black Tea Custard:
   - In a saucepan, combine heavy cream, milk, and 1/4 cup sugar. Warm over medium heat until the mixture is hot but not boiling.
   - Add the black tea leaves or tea bags to the hot cream mixture. Remove from heat, cover, and let steep for 10-15 minutes to infuse the cream with the tea flavor.
   - In a separate bowl, whisk together egg yolks and an additional 1/4 cup sugar until the mixture is light and fluffy.
   - Remove the tea leaves or bags from the cream mixture, squeezing out any excess liquid.
   - Gradually pour the warm tea-infused cream into the egg yolk mixture, whisking constantly to prevent the eggs from scrambling.
   - Return the combined mixture to the saucepan and heat over low heat, stirring continuously, until the custard thickens enough to coat the back of a spoon (about 170°F on a cooking thermometer).
   - Stir in vanilla extract, then strain the custard through a fine-mesh sieve to ensure it is smooth.

Instructions Continued:

3. Assemble and Chill:
   - Pour the custard into the prepared ginger snap crust.
   - Chill in the refrigerator for at least 4 hours, or until the custard is set and firm.

4. Serve:
   - Cut into slices and serve chilled. Garnish with a sprinkle of crushed ginger snaps or a dollop of whipped cream if desired.

Thai Chili Chocolate Mousse

Difficulty: Medium

Flavor Profile: This dessert merges the luxurious richness of chocolate mousse with the exciting kick of Thai chili, creating a unique and sophisticated sweet treat that delights with every spoonful. It's a perfect blend of heat, sweet, and silky textures.

This Thai Chili Chocolate Mousse offers a delightful surprise to the palate, blending the familiar decadence of chocolate with the exotic heat of Thai chili, making it an unforgettable dessert experience.

Tips:

- Chocolate Quality: Use high-quality chocolate as it's the primary flavor carrier in this dessert. The better the chocolate, the richer and more profound the mousse.
- Handling Egg Whites: Ensure no yolk gets into the whites and that the beaters and bowl are perfectly clean and dry to achieve the best volume.
- Introducing Heat: Start with a conservative amount of chili powder, as it can overpower the other flavors. You can always add more to the whipped cream topping for those who prefer a spicier taste.
- Serving Suggestions: For an extra special presentation, serve with a side of shortbread cookies or a light, crisp biscotti which complements the soft texture of the mousse.

Ingredients:

- *For the Chocolate Mousse:*
  - 8 ounces semi-sweet chocolate, finely chopped
  - 2 tablespoons unsalted butter
  - 1/4 teaspoon Thai chili powder (adjust based on heat preference)
  - 1/2 teaspoon ground cinnamon
  - 3 large eggs, separated
  - 1/4 cup granulated sugar
  - 1 cup heavy cream
  - 1 teaspoon vanilla extract

- *For Garnish:*
  - Whipped cream
  - Shaved chocolate
  - A light dusting of chili powder or finely minced fresh Thai chili for extra heat (optional)

Instructions:

1. Prepare the Chocolate Base:
    - Combine chopped chocolate, butter, Thai chili powder, and ground cinnamon in a heatproof bowl.
    - Set the bowl over a pot of simmering water (double boiler), ensuring the bottom does not touch the water. Stir continuously until the chocolate and butter melt together smoothly. Remove from heat and let cool slightly.

2. Mix Egg Yolks:
    - In a small bowl, whisk the egg yolks with 2 tablespoons of sugar until the mixture is pale and thick. Gradually fold this into the melted chocolate mixture until well combined. Set aside.

3. Whip Egg Whites:
    - In a clean, dry bowl, beat the egg whites until soft peaks form. Gradually add the remaining sugar, continuing to beat until stiff peaks form.
    - Gently fold the egg whites into the chocolate mixture, taking care not to deflate the mixture, ensuring it's evenly incorporated.

4. Whip Cream:
    - In another bowl, whip the heavy cream with vanilla extract until it forms soft peaks. Carefully fold the whipped cream into the chocolate mixture until no white streaks remain. This is your mousse.

Instructions Continued:

5. Chill the Mousse:

    - Pour the mousse into individual serving dishes or a large serving bowl. Refrigerate for at least 4 hours, or overnight, until set.

6. Serve:

    - Top each serving with a dollop of whipped cream, a sprinkle of shaved chocolate, and a tiny dusting of chili powder or fresh minced chili if desired for extra heat and visual appeal.

Blackberry Bao with Cream Cheese Filling

Difficulty: Medium

Flavor Profile: This dessert offers a unique blend of the soft, pillowy texture of traditional bao buns filled with a creamy, tart blackberry and cream cheese mixture. It merges the tangy, fruity flavors with the sweet, smooth richness of cream cheese, all encased in a warm, steamed bun.

Blackberry Bao with Cream Cheese Filling creatively combines traditional Asian techniques with Western flavors, offering a sweet twist on a classic that is sure to impress.

Tips:

- Dough Consistency: If the dough is too sticky, add a little more flour; if it's too dry, add a few drops of milk. The dough should be soft and pliable.
- Filling Tips: Ensure the filling is not too runny as it may leak during steaming. If the jam is very liquid, reduce it on the stovetop to thicken it before mixing with the cream cheese.
- Steaming: Do not overcrowd the steamer. Steam the bao in batches if necessary to ensure they cook evenly and expand properly without sticking together.
- Serving Suggestions: These bao are best enjoyed warm when the filling is creamy and the dough is soft. They can be a unique dessert after a meal or a delightful snack on their own.

Ingredients:

- For the Bao Dough:
  - 2 cups all-purpose flour
  - 1/4 cup sugar
  - 1/2 teaspoon salt
  - 1 tablespoon baking powder
  - 1 teaspoon instant yeast
  - 3/4 cup warm milk

- For the Filling:
  - 8 ounces cream cheese, softened
  - 1/2 cup blackberry jam
  - 1/4 cup fresh blackberries, chopped
  - 1 tablespoon lemon zest
  - 2 tablespoons granulated sugar

- For Garnish:
  - Powdered sugar for dusting
  - Additional whole blackberries

Instructions:

1. Prepare the Bao Dough:
   - In a large mixing bowl, combine flour, sugar, salt, baking powder, and yeast. Gradually add warm milk to the dry ingredients, stirring until a soft dough forms.
   - Turn the dough out onto a lightly floured surface and knead until smooth and elastic, about 10 minutes.
   - Place the dough in a greased bowl, cover with a damp cloth, and let rise in a warm place until doubled in size, about 1 hour.

2. Make the Cream Cheese Filling:
   - In a mixing bowl, beat together the softened cream cheese, blackberry jam, chopped blackberries, lemon zest, and granulated sugar until well combined. The mixture should be creamy but with small chunks of berries for texture.

Instructions Continued:

3. Assemble the Bao:
   - Once the dough has risen, punch it down and turn it out onto a floured surface. Divide the dough into 12 equal pieces.
   - Roll each piece into a ball, then flatten into a disk about 4 inches in diameter.
   - Place a tablespoon of the cream cheese filling in the center of each disk. Gather the edges of the dough over the filling, pinching them together to seal.
   - Place each filled bun seam-side down on a small piece of parchment paper.

4. Steam the Bao:
   - Prepare your steamer by bringing water to a simmer. Place buns with their parchment squares in the steamer basket, making sure they do not touch as they will expand. Cover and steam for about 12-15 minutes, or until the bao is puffed and the surface is smooth.
   - Remove the buns from the steamer and let them cool slightly on a wire rack.

5. Serve:
   - Dust the warm bao with powdered sugar and garnish with fresh blackberries right before serving.

Matcha Cloud Bread with Sorghum Syrup

Difficulty: Easy

Flavor Profile: This light, airy cloud bread is subtly flavored with earthy matcha and drizzled with rich Southern sorghum syrup. It's a unique fusion of Japanese and Southern flavors that creates a fun and delicious treat

This Matcha Cloud Bread with Sorghum Syrup is a fun, light, and delicious dessert that combines the airy texture of cloud bread with the earthy matcha flavor and the deep sweetness of Southern sorghum syrup. It's perfect for a quick treat or an impressive, unique dessert for guests!

Tips:
- Whipping Egg Whites: Ensure that your mixing bowl and beaters are completely clean and dry before whipping the egg whites. Any trace of grease or moisture can prevent the egg whites from whipping properly.
- Folding Technique: Gently fold the matcha and cornstarch into the egg whites to avoid deflating the mixture. Use a slow, circular motion with the spatula for best results.
- Sorghum Syrup: If sorghum syrup is too thick for your liking, feel free to dilute it with a bit of warm water to make it easier to drizzle. Its rich, earthy sweetness pairs wonderfully with the matcha flavor.

Ingredients:

- For the Cloud Bread:
- 3 large egg whites
- 2 1/2 tablespoons white sugar
- 1 tablespoon cornstarch
- 1 teaspoon matcha powder (culinary grade)
- 1/2 teaspoon vanilla extract (optional)
- A pinch of salt

- For the Sorghum Syrup Drizzle:
- 1/4 cup sorghum syrup (you can substitute with maple syrup if unavailable)
- 1 tablespoon warm water (optional, to thin the syrup)

Instructions:

1. Preheat the Oven:
   - Preheat your oven to 300°F (150°C). Line a baking sheet with parchment paper or a silicone baking mat.

2. Whip the Egg Whites:
   - In a clean, grease-free mixing bowl, beat the egg whites with a pinch of salt using an electric mixer on medium speed. Continue beating until the egg whites become frothy.
   - Gradually add the sugar, 1 tablespoon at a time, while continuing to beat the egg whites on high speed.
   - Once all the sugar is added, continue whipping the egg whites until stiff peaks form and the mixture is glossy.

3. Incorporate the Matcha:
   - In a small bowl, sift the cornstarch and matcha powder together to remove any clumps.
   - Gently fold the matcha and cornstarch mixture into the whipped egg whites using a spatula. Be careful not to deflate the egg whites too much. Fold in the vanilla extract, if using.

4. Shape the Cloud Bread:
   - Scoop the matcha-infused egg white mixture onto the prepared baking sheet, shaping it into a dome or cloud-like mound. Smooth out the surface with the back of a spoon or spatula.

Instructions Continued:

5. Bake the Cloud Bread:
- Bake in the preheated oven for 20-25 minutes, or until the cloud bread is set, slightly golden, and firm on the outside but soft and airy on the inside.

6. Prepare the Sorghum Syrup:
- In a small bowl, whisk together the sorghum syrup and 1 tablespoon of warm water if you prefer a thinner consistency for drizzling. Adjust the thickness to your liking.

7. Serve:
- Once the cloud bread has cooled slightly, transfer it to a serving plate.
- Drizzle generously with the sorghum syrup for a rich, sweet finish. You can also sprinkle a little extra matcha powder on top for presentation, if desired.

Yuzu Honey Cake with Lavender Frosting

Difficulty: Medium

Flavor Profile: This dessert combines the bright, citrusy notes of yuzu with the natural sweetness of honey and the aromatic elegance of lavender frosting, creating a sophisticated and unique cake perfect for special occasions.

Yuzu Honey Cake with Lavender Frosting offers a delightful blend of citrus, sweet, and floral flavors, making it an ideal choice for those who appreciate cakes that are as aromatic as they are delicious.

Tips:
- Cake Texture: For a lighter cake, ensure not to overmix the batter once the flour is added.
- Lavender Flavor: If ground lavender flowers are too intense or difficult to find, you can infuse the milk with whole lavender flowers. Heat the milk with the lavender, then strain and cool before using.
- Yuzu Juice: Yuzu can be tart; adjust the amount of honey or sugar if you prefer a sweeter cake.
- Storage: This cake keeps well covered at room temperature for a day; for longer storage, refrigerate it and bring to room temperature before serving.

Ingredients:

- *For the Yuzu Honey Cake:*
  - 2 1/2 cups all-purpose flour
  - 2 teaspoons baking powder
  - 1/2 teaspoon salt
  - 3/4 cup unsalted butter, room temperature
  - 1 cup granulated sugar
  - 1/2 cup honey
  - 4 large eggs
  - 1 tablespoon yuzu zest
  - 1/4 cup yuzu juice
  - 1/2 cup buttermilk

- *For the Lavender Frosting:*
  - 1 cup unsalted butter, softened
  - 3 to 4 cups powdered sugar, sifted
  - 1 tablespoon dried lavender flowers, finely ground
  - 2 tablespoons milk
  - 1 teaspoon vanilla extract

- *For Garnish:*
  - Fresh lavender sprigs
  - Additional yuzu zest

Instructions:

1. Prepare the Yuzu Honey Cake:
   - Preheat your oven to 350°F (175°C). Grease and flour two 8-inch round cake pans and line the bottoms with parchment paper.
   - In a medium bowl, whisk together flour, baking powder, and salt. Set aside.
   - In a large mixing bowl, cream the butter, granulated sugar, and honey until light and fluffy. Beat in the eggs one at a time, fully incorporating each before adding the next.
   - Mix in yuzu zest and yuzu juice.
   - Alternately add the flour mixture and buttermilk to the creamed mixture, starting and ending with the flour. Mix until just combined.
   - Divide the batter evenly between the prepared pans. Bake for 25-30 minutes, or until a toothpick inserted into the center comes out clean.
   - Allow the cakes to cool in the pans for 10 minutes, then turn out onto wire racks to cool completely.

Instructions Continued:

2. Make the Lavender Frosting:
    - In a mixing bowl, beat the softened butter until smooth and creamy. Gradually add powdered sugar, one cup at a time, beating well on medium speed. Scrape sides and bottom of the bowl often.
    - Once all the sugar has been mixed in, the frosting will appear dry. Add milk, vanilla extract, and ground lavender flowers. Beat at high speed until frosting is smooth and creamy.

3. Assemble the Cake:
    - Place one cake layer on a serving plate. Spread a layer of lavender frosting over the top.
    - Top with the second cake layer and apply a thin crumb coat over the entire cake. Chill for 15-20 minutes to set the frosting.
    - After the crumb coat is set, continue frosting the cake with the remaining lavender frosting, smoothing the sides and top.

4. Garnish and Serve:
    - Decorate with fresh lavender sprigs and sprinkle some yuzu zest over the top for added color and flavor.
    - Serve the cake at room temperature for best flavor and texture.

Rice Paper "Peach Cobbler" Rolls

Difficulty: Medium

Flavor Profile: This innovative take on a Southern peach cobbler uses rice paper soaked in egg instead of a traditional pie crust, forming crispy rolls filled with spiced peaches.

These Southern desserts reinvent traditional favorites by substituting egg-soaked rice paper for classic dough or crust, resulting in a light, crispy texture with a unique twist.

Tips:

- Rice Paper Handling: Soak the rice paper just until soft. Over-soaking can make it too delicate and difficult to handle.
- Egg Mixture: Ensure the rice paper is fully coated in the egg mixture to help it fry to a crispy, golden brown texture.
- Frying Temperature: Maintain a steady frying temperature of around 350°F to achieve even crispiness without burning the rice paper.

Ingredients:

- 12 sheets of rice paper
- 2 large eggs
- 1/2 cup milk

Ingredients Continued:

- 1 tablespoon sugar
- 3 large peaches, peeled and sliced
- 1/4 cup brown sugar
- 1 teaspoon cinnamon
- 1/4 teaspoon nutmeg
- 1 tablespoon cornstarch
- Vegetable oil for frying
- Whipped cream or vanilla ice cream, for serving

Instructions:

1. Prepare the Egg Mixture:
    - In a bowl, whisk together the eggs, milk, and sugar.

2. Cook the Peaches:
    - In a saucepan, combine the sliced peaches, brown sugar, cinnamon, nutmeg, and cornstarch.
    - Cook over medium heat for 5-7 minutes, until the peaches soften and the mixture thickens slightly.
    - Remove from heat and let cool slightly.

3. Soak and Fill the Rice Paper:
    - Submerge one sheet of rice paper at a time in warm water for 5-10 seconds to soften.
    - Gently place the softened rice paper onto a flat surface, then dip it into the egg mixture, ensuring both sides are coated.
    - Place about 2 tablespoons of the spiced peach mixture onto the center of the rice paper.
    - Fold the sides over the filling and roll it up like a spring roll, tucking in the edges to seal.

4. Fry the Rolls:
    - Heat about 1 inch of vegetable oil in a skillet or deep fryer over medium heat until it reaches 350°F (175°C).
    - Fry the rolls in batches, cooking for 2-3 minutes on each side until golden brown and crispy.
    - Remove from the oil and drain on a paper towel-lined plate.

5. Serve:
    - Serve the rice paper "peach cobbler" rolls warm, alongside whipped cream or a scoop of vanilla ice cream for a delicious twist on the classic Southern dessert.

Blueberry Lychee Cobbler

Difficulty: Medium

Flavor Profile: This dessert brings together the sweet and tart flavors of blueberries with the exotic, floral notes of lychees, covered with a soft, biscuity topping. It's a unique fusion that combines traditional Southern cobbler with a touch of Asian flair.

This Blueberry Lychee Cobbler is a delightful twist on a classic, introducing a taste of the tropics to a beloved Southern dessert. The combination of blueberries and lychees offers a refreshing balance of flavors, perfect for a summer treat or a special occasion dessert.

Tips:
- Fruit Consistency: If using canned lychees, drain them well to prevent excess moisture from making the filling too runny.
- Handling the Dough: Be careful not to overwork the cobbler topping dough to keep it light and fluffy.
- Baking: Place a baking sheet under the baking dish to catch any drips from the fruit as it bubbles.
- Storage: Leftover cobbler can be stored in the refrigerator for up to 3 days and reheated in the oven or microwave.

Ingredients:

- *For the Fruit Filling:*
  - 2 cups fresh blueberries
  - 1 cup lychees, peeled, pitted, and roughly chopped (canned lychees can be used if fresh are unavailable)
  - 1/2 cup granulated sugar
  - 2 tablespoons cornstarch
  - Juice of 1 lemon
  - 1 teaspoon vanilla extract

- *For the Cobbler Topping:*
  - 1 cup all-purpose flour
  - 1/4 cup granulated sugar
  - 1/4 cup brown sugar
  - 1 teaspoon baking powder
  - 1/2 teaspoon salt
  - 6 tablespoons unsalted butter, cold and cubed
  - 1/4 cup boiling water

- *Additional*:
  - Ice cream or whipped cream, for serving
  - Fresh mint, for garnish

Instructions:

1. Prepare the Fruit Filling:
    - Preheat your oven to 375°F (190°C).
    - In a large bowl, combine blueberries and lychees with granulated sugar, cornstarch, lemon juice, and vanilla extract. Toss gently to coat the fruit evenly.
    - Pour the fruit mixture into an 8-inch square baking dish, spreading it out evenly.

2. Make the Cobbler Topping:
    - In a medium bowl, mix together flour, granulated sugar, brown sugar, baking powder, and salt.
    - Add cold, cubed butter to the flour mixture. Using a pastry blender or your fingertips, blend the butter into the flour until the mixture resembles coarse crumbs.
    - Stir in boiling water just until the mixture is just combined and moistened.

Instructions Continued:

3. Assemble and Bake the Cobbler:
    - Spoon the topping over the fruit mixture in the baking dish. The topping should be rough and crumbly to allow steam to escape and the fruit mixture to bubble through.
    - Place the dish in the preheated oven and bake for about 35-45 minutes, or until the topping is golden brown and the fruit filling is bubbly.

4. Serve:
    - Serve the cobbler warm or at room temperature. It pairs wonderfully with a scoop of vanilla ice cream or a dollop of whipped cream.
    - Garnish with fresh mint leaves to enhance the flavors and add a touch of color.

DRINKS

Rice-Washed Cocktail Base

Flavor Profile: The rice-washing technique imparts a smooth, creamy mouthfeel and subtle nuttiness to these classic cocktails, adding depth and a unique twist to each drink. The rice complements the spirit-forward nature of the drinks, softening the edges and enhancing the flavors without overwhelming them.

Ingredients:
- 1 cup cooked jasmine rice (or any aromatic rice)
- 750 ml bottle of gin, bourbon, whiskey, or vodka (depending on the cocktail variation)
- 1 cup water

Instructions:

1. Cook the Rice:
   - Cook 1 cup of jasmine rice according to the package instructions, but omit any seasoning, salt, or butter.
   - Allow the rice to cool to room temperature.

2. Combine with Spirit:
   - In a large, clean container or jar, combine the cooked rice with 1 cup of water and your choice of 750 ml spirit (gin for Negroni and Martini; bourbon or whiskey for Manhattan and Old Fashioned).
   - Stir gently to ensure the rice is evenly distributed in the liquid.

3. Infuse:
   - Let the rice and spirit mixture infuse at room temperature for 1-2 hours, stirring occasionally to extract the subtle starches and aromatics from the rice.
   - After 2 hours, strain the mixture through a fine mesh sieve or cheesecloth to remove the rice solids, leaving only the rice-washed spirit.

4. Store:
   - The rice-washed spirit can be stored in a sealed bottle in the fridge for up to one week. It's now ready to be used in your cocktail variations!

Tips:

- Rice Choice: Jasmine rice adds a subtle floral note, but other varieties like basmati or sushi rice can be used for different flavor profiles.
- Infusion Time: Don't let the rice-washing process exceed 2 hours, as it may introduce too much starch and make the texture too thick.
- Adjust Sweetness: For cocktails like the Old Fashioned, you can adjust the sweetness to your liking by altering the amount of sugar used.

Rice-Washed Negroni

Flavor Profile: Smooth, slightly creamy, with bitter and citrus notes softened by the rice-washed gin.

Ingredients:
- 1 oz rice-washed gin
- 1 oz Campari
- 1 oz sweet vermouth
- Orange peel, for garnish

Instructions:
1. Add the rice-washed gin, Campari, and sweet vermouth to a mixing glass filled with ice.
2. Stir until well chilled, about 30 seconds.
3. Strain into a rocks glass filled with ice.
4. Garnish with an orange peel.

Rice-Washed Manhattan

Flavor Profile: A softened, nutty, and slightly creamy version of the classic Manhattan with a smooth rice-washed bourbon or rye.

Ingredients:

- 2 oz rice-washed bourbon or rye whiskey
- 1 oz sweet vermouth
- 2 dashes Angostura bitters
- Cherry, for garnish

Instructions:

1. Combine the rice-washed bourbon, sweet vermouth, and bitters in a mixing glass with ice.
2. Stir for about 30 seconds until well chilled.
3. Strain into a chilled coupe or martini glass.
4. Garnish with a cherry.

Rice-Washed Martini

Flavor Profile: Clean and smooth, the rice-washed gin softens the traditional sharpness of the martini.

Ingredients:
- 2 oz rice-washed gin
- 1/2 oz dry vermouth
- Lemon twist or olive, for garnish

Instructions:
1. Combine the rice-washed gin and dry vermouth in a mixing glass filled with ice.
2. Stir until well chilled, about 30 seconds.
3. Strain into a chilled martini glass.
4. Garnish with a lemon twist or olive.

Rice-Washed Old Fashioned

Flavor Profile: A mellow, creamy version of the Old Fashioned, with rice-washed bourbon providing a smoother base.

Ingredients:
- 2 oz rice-washed bourbon
- 1 sugar cube
- 2 dashes Angostura bitters
- Orange peel, for garnish

Instructions:
1. Muddle the sugar cube and bitters in a rocks glass.
2. Add the rice-washed bourbon and stir to dissolve the sugar.
3. Fill the glass with a large ice cube and stir until chilled.
4. Garnish with an orange peel.

Green Tea Mint Julep

Flavor Profile: The classic Southern charm of a mint julep with a hint of earthy green tea.

Ingredients:
- 2 oz bourbon
- 1 oz green tea, brewed strong and chilled (Can be substituted for 1/2 tsp matcha powder)
- 1/2 oz simple syrup
- Fresh mint leaves
- Crushed ice

Instructions:

1. Muddle Mint: In a chilled julep cup, gently muddle mint leaves with simple syrup to release their oils.
2. Mix Drink: Add bourbon and green tea. Fill the glass with crushed ice and stir well until the cup is frosted.
3. Garnish and Serve: Garnish with a sprig of mint and serve immediately.

Sake Sangria

Flavor Profile: A fruity and refreshing twist on traditional sangria with a sake base.

Ingredients:
- 1 bottle of sake
- 1/2 cup peach liqueur
- 2 cups mixed fresh fruit (oranges, lemons, limes, berries)
- 2 tablespoons sugar
- Club soda, to top
- Ice

Instructions:

1.   Prepare Fruit: Slice citrus fruits into thin rounds and berries in halves.

2.   Mix Sangria: In a pitcher, combine sake, peach liqueur, sliced fruits, and sugar. Stir until sugar is dissolved.

3.   Chill: Refrigerate for at least 4 hours to allow flavors to meld.

4.   Serve: Fill glasses with ice, pour sangria over, and top with a splash of club soda.

Lemongrass-Ginger Sweet Tea

Flavor Profile: A Southern sweet tea infused with aromatic lemongrass and spicy ginger.

Ingredients:
- 4 cups water
- 4 black tea bags
- 1 stalk lemongrass, cut into pieces and bruised
- 1-inch piece of ginger, thinly sliced
- 1/2 cup sugar

Instructions:
1. Simmer: In a saucepan, bring water, lemongrass, and ginger to a boil. Remove from heat, add tea bags, and steep for 5 minutes.
2. Sweeten: Remove tea bags, add sugar, and stir until dissolved.
3. Cool and Serve: Strain the tea into a pitcher, discarding solids. Refrigerate until cold. Serve over ice.

Lychee-Lavender Lemonade

Flavor Profile: Sweet lychee and aromatic lavender pair beautifully in this refreshing lemonade.

Ingredients:
- 1 cup lychee juice (from canned lychees)
- 4 cups cold water
- 3/4 cup lemon juice
- 1/2 cup sugar
- 2 teaspoons dried lavender flowers

Instructions:

1. Infuse Lavender: In a small saucepan, heat 1 cup of water and lavender flowers until hot but not boiling. Remove from heat, cover, and let steep for 10 minutes. Strain and discard lavender.

2. Mix Lemonade: In a pitcher, combine lychee juice, infused lavender water, remaining water, lemon juice, and sugar. Stir until sugar is dissolved.

3. Chill and Serve: Refrigerate until chilled. Serve over ice and garnish with lychee fruit if desired.

Spiced Plum Iced Tea

Flavor Profile: Juicy plums and aromatic spices make this iced tea a unique treat.

Ingredients:
- 6 cups water
- 4 black tea bags
- 4 plums, pitted and sliced
- 1 cinnamon stick
- 2 star anise
- 1/4 cup honey

Instructions:

1.   Simmer Plums and Spices: In a saucepan, bring water, plums, cinnamon, and star anise to a boil. Reduce heat and simmer for 5 minutes.

2.   Steep Tea: Add tea bags, remove from heat, and steep for 5 minutes. Remove tea bags.

3.   Sweeten and Chill: Stir in honey until dissolved. Strain the mixture into a pitcher, discarding solids. Refrigerate until cold.

4.   Serve: Pour over ice and garnish with a slice of plum or a cinnamon stick.

Yuzu Whiskey Sour

Flavor Profile: The tartness of yuzu blends with the smoothness of bourbon in this twist on a classic cocktail.

Ingredients:
- 2 oz bourbon
- 1 oz yuzu juice (or substitute with a mix of lemon and lime juice)
- 1/2 oz simple syrup
- Ice
- Angostura bitters, optional

Instructions:
1. Combine Ingredients: In a shaker, combine bourbon, yuzu juice, simple syrup, and ice.
2. Shake: Shake well until the outside of the shaker is frosted.
3. Serve: Strain into an old-fashioned glass filled with ice. Add a dash of bitters if desired.

Coconut Water Mojito

Flavor Profile: A tropical version of the mojito with refreshing coconut water and mint.

Ingredients:
- 1/2 lime, cut into wedges
- 6-8 mint leaves
- 1 tbsp sugar
- 2 oz white rum
- 4 oz coconut water
- Ice
- Sparkling water, to top
- Additional mint, for garnish

Instructions:
1. Muddle: In a sturdy glass, muddle lime wedges with sugar and mint leaves to release the lime juice and mint oils.
2. Mix: Add rum and coconut water. Fill the glass with ice.
3. Top and Serve: Top with sparkling water. Stir well and garnish with more mint.

Tamarind Margarita

Flavor Profile: A tangy and sweet tamarind paste gives a new life to the classic margarita.

Ingredients:
- 2 oz tequila
- 1 oz tamarind paste, dissolved in a little warm water
- 1/2 oz triple sec
- 1 oz lime juice
- Salt for rimming
- Ice

Instructions:

1. Prepare Glass: Rim a margarita glass with lime juice and dip in salt.
2. Mix Drink: In a shaker, combine tequila, diluted tamarind paste, triple sec, lime juice, and ice.
3. Shake and Serve: Shake well and strain into the prepared glass. Add ice if desired.

Glossary

Asian Ingredients

Gochujang (Korean Chili Paste)
- Description: A savory, sweet, and spicy fermented condiment made from chili powder, glutinous rice, fermented soybeans, and salt.
- Substitutions: For a gluten-free alternative, use tamari-based chili paste. For less heat, mix red pepper flakes with miso paste.

Miso Paste
- Description: A traditional Japanese seasoning produced by fermenting soybeans with salt and koji.
- Substitutions: For soy allergies, chickpea miso can be used. For a simpler substitute in soups or marinades, use a mixture of soy sauce and a pinch of tahini.

Kaffir Lime Leaves
- Description: Used in Thai cooking, these leaves add a strong citrus flavor to food.
- Substitutions: If unavailable, use a combination of bay leaf and lime zest to mimic the flavor.

Sesame Oil
- Description: the edible oil extracted from the seeds of Sesamum indicum. Sesame oil is used as a cooking oil and as a food ingredient
- Substitutions: Perilla Oil originates in Korean cooking and has a similar nutty flavor and can be used a substitution for those with a sesame allergy

Daikon Radish
- Description: A mild-flavored winter radish commonly used in Japanese and Korean cuisine, often pickled or added to soups.
- Substitutions: White turnips or jicama can be used as a crunchier alternative with a similar mild taste.

Shiso Leaves
- Description: An aromatic Japanese herb with a flavor that's a cross between mint and basil.
- Substitutions: A mix of basil and mint can mimic shiso's unique flavor in recipes.

Black Vinegar

- Description: A dark, complex vinegar made from grains, popular in Chinese cuisine, especially in braised dishes and as a dipping sauce component.
- Substitutions: Balsamic vinegar mixed with a little soy sauce can substitute for its depth and acidity.

Yuzu

- Description: A citrus fruit from East Asia known for its distinct aroma, used for its zest and juice.
- Substitutions: A combination of lemon zest, lime juice, and a hint of orange captures a similar flavor profile.

Mirin

- Description: A sweet Japanese cooking wine essential for many sauces and glazes.
- Substitutions: A mix of white wine and a dash of sugar or honey can be used when mirin is unavailable.

Galangal

- Description: A root similar to ginger but with a sharper, citrusy taste, commonly used in Thai cooking.
- Substitutions: Ginger mixed with a pinch of lemon zest can be used, though the flavor will be milder.

Thai Basil

- Description: A variety of basil that has a spicy, licorice-like flavor, used extensively in Thai cuisine.
- Substitutions: Regular basil may be used, though it lacks the spice; consider adding a small amount of anise or licorice root.

Szechuan Peppercorns

- Description: Not true peppercorns but the outer pod of the tiny fruit of a tree from the prickly ash family, known for their numbing effect in Chinese cuisine.
- Substitutions: Combine ground black peppercorns and coriander seeds for a similar aroma, minus the numbing effect.

Fish Sauce

- Description: A pungent, salty sauce made from fermented fish, used in Southeast Asian cooking to add umami.
- Substitutions: Worcestershire sauce or soy sauce mixed with a pinch of salt can be used, though they are less pungent.

Tamarind Paste

- Description: A sour paste made from the fruit of the tamarind tree, used in Indian and Southeast Asian cuisine.
- Substitutions: A mixture of lemon juice and brown sugar can mimic its sour-sweet profile.

Southern Ingredients

Andouille Sausage
- Description: A spicy, smoked pork sausage, prominent in Cajun cuisine.
- Substitutions: For a less fatty or non-pork version, use chicken or turkey sausage seasoned with cayenne and paprika.

Sorghum Syrup
- Description: A sweet syrup made from the sorghum plant, used in Southern cooking for baking and as a condiment.
- Substitutions: Molasses or honey can substitute, though they are sweeter and lack the distinct tang of sorghum.

Vidalia Onion
- Description: A sweet onion variety grown in Georgia, known for its mild flavor, making it ideal for frying and salads.
- Substitutions: Other sweet onion varieties like Walla Walla or Maui can be used.

Blackstrap Molasses
- Description: A dark, viscous molasses with a bittersweet flavor, a byproduct of sugar cane's refining process, used in robust sauces and baking.
- Substitutions: Dark corn syrup mixed with a touch of bittersweet chocolate can be used in baking.

Molasses
- Description: A viscous product resulting from refining sugarcane or sugar beets into sugar, used in baking and sauces.
- Substitutions: For a lower glycemic index, use date syrup or honey in equal measure.

Grits
- Description: Made from stone-ground corn, used in a variety of Southern dishes, from breakfast to dinner.
- Substitutions: Polenta or coarse ground cornmeal, though they may cook differently.

Country Ham
- Description: A salty, cured ham aged for flavor, often served in thin slices or used to flavor dishes like greens or beans.
- Substitutions: Prosciutto or other dry-cured hams, though milder, can be used with an adjustment for saltiness.

Collard Greens
- Description: A type of kale, slow-cooked with ham hocks or bacon, a staple in Southern cuisine.
- Substitutions: Mustard greens or Swiss chard can be used, though they have a sharper flavor.

Pecans
- Description: A type of nut native to the Southern U.S., used in desserts like pecan pie or savory dishes like stuffing.
- Substitutions: Walnuts or almonds, though they lack the sweetness and buttery texture of pecans.

Hot Sauce
- Description: A spicy sauce made from peppers, vinegar, and salt, used to add heat to Southern dishes.
- Substitutions: Cayenne pepper mixed with vinegar can be used to achieve similar heat levels.

Cornmeal
- Description: Made from dried corn, it's a base for Southern staples like cornbread and hushpuppies.
- Substitutions: For a gluten-free option, ensure the cornmeal is labeled as such, as cross-contamination is common. Otherwise, ground oats can sometimes be used.

Cornbread
- Description: A type of bread made from cornmeal, often baked or fried, a Southern staple.
- Substitutions: Other grain breads can be used, though they lack the distinctive texture and flavor of cornbread.

Bourbon
- Description: A type of American whiskey, key in many Southern dishes and sauces.
- Substitutions: For alcohol-free recipes, use apple cider vinegar mixed with vanilla extract for a similar flavor profile.

Fried Green Tomatoes
- Description: Unripe tomatoes coated in cornmeal and fried, a Southern classic.
- Substitutions: Green tomatillos can be used for a similar tartness but should be sliced thicker.

Okra
- Description: A vegetable used in gumbo and stews or fried on its own.
- Substitutions: Zucchini or eggplant can be used in stews, though they lack okra's thickening properties.

Biscuits

- Description: Flaky, buttery bread rolls that are a staple of Southern breakfasts and dinners.
- Substitutions: Scones or plain dinner rolls can substitute, though they have a different texture.

Creole Mustard

- Description: A grainy mustard with a sharp flavor, used in Cajun and Creole cooking.
- Substitutions: Whole grain Dijon mustard mixed with a touch of horseradish can approximate the flavor.

Cane Syrup

- Description: Made from sugarcane, it's thick and sweet, used in baking and sauces.
- Substitutions: Dark corn syrup or golden syrup can substitute, though they are milder.

Red Eye Gravy

- Description: A savory gravy made from coffee and the drippings of cooked ham.
- Substitutions: Beef broth mixed with a touch of instant coffee can mimic its deep flavor.

Catfish

- Description: A freshwater fish that's a staple in Southern fried dishes.
- Substitutions: Tilapia or other mild, white freshwater fish can be used.

Hoecake

- Description: A cornmeal flatbread, cooked originally on a hoe's blade over a fire, similar to cornbread.
- Substitutions: Polenta cakes or plain cornbread are the closest alternatives.

Sweet Tea

- Description: Iced tea sweetened with sugar, sometimes flavored with lemon or mint, a ubiquitous Southern refreshment.
- Substitutions: Honey-sweetened iced tea with a splash of lemon can be used for a similar refreshing drink.

Hushpuppies

- Description: Small, round cornmeal breads, deep-fried, often served with fried fish.
- Substitutions: Deep-fried mini muffins can offer a similar texture and taste

Made in the USA
Columbia, SC
12 October 2024

3471f7ac-4419-443b-9e35-49223f800c68R01